# The Würzburg residence and court gardens

Official guide

Edited by
Erich Bachmann,
Burkard von Roda
and
Werner Helmberger

Bayerische
Schlösserverwaltung

# CONTENTS

*Putto on the stove of the White Hall (Room 4)*

4

# Architectural and Artistic Significance

Unlike the royal Residence in Munich, which evolved over some five hundred years and thus incorporates the styles of quite different periods, the Würzburg Residence was built almost within a single generation. The significance of this great building is not therefore the vertical line of tradition, but rather the homogeneity of its style, the horizontal coherence and the breadth of artistic vision. The architects in fact drew their inspiration from an area extending from Vienna to Paris and from Genoa and Venice to Amsterdam. The building embodies the attainments of Western architecture of its day, the foremost contemporary trends in French château architecture, Viennese imperial baroque and the religious and secular architecture of northern Italy, and is a synthesis of the arts of astonishing universality. No palace or castle, either in Germany or in the Latin countries, can surpass the Würzburg Residence for its masterful combination of many different western styles. Major artists from the principal artistic regions of Europe collaborated on the building. The Würzburg court architect, Balthasar Neumann, who was entrusted with the coordination of the building plans, had to work not only with the leading German and French architects such as the imperial court architect in Vienna, Lucas von Hildebrandt, the architect of the Elector of Mainz, Maximilian von Welsch, as well as the haughty Robert de Cotte, »architecte du Roy et inspecteur general«, und Germain Boffrand in Paris, but also with artists such as Antonio Bossi, the »ornamental genius« of the Würzburg Residence, the gifted sculptors and woodcarvers Johann Wolfgang van der Auvera from

*»... it must surely be the most beautiful (palace) in Germany. The staircase is wonderful.«*

Margravine Wilhelmine of Bayreuth

*View of the Imperial Hall pavilion of the Residence from the East Garden*

Mecheln and Georg Adam Guthmann from Munich, and last but not least the greatest fresco painter of the 18th century, Giovanni Battista Tiepolo. These artists and craftsmen decorated and furnished Balthasar Neumann's incomparable sequence of rooms – vestibule, staircase, White Hall and Imperial Hall – one of the most magnificent in the history of palace architecture. In addition, this joint creative achievement also produced »Würzburg rococo«, the most exuberant of all the variations of this style in Germany. The Würzburg Residence is a work of art of unique importance in the history of architecture, in some respects marking the culmination of the European baroque style, and in its particular form could only have been produced in Germany, and here in fact only in Franconia.

The Würzburg Residence is moreover by no means the work of the artists alone, but equally that of its various great owners, who in addition to providing the financial and political means put this gigantic building on an international level through their widespread connections. These were the Counts of Schönborn. For several generations, members of this extensive, gifted family resided frequently and sometimes even simultaneously in a number of ecclesiastical principalities: for example in Würzburg, Bamberg and also in Mainz, Worms, Speyer and Trier. As a result, just before the fall of the Holy Roman Empire this considerable territory in the middle of Germany became a thriving political and cultural center, without which the history of German baroque architecture would be inconceivable. Under the leadership of this house, Franconia built the best palaces in Germany and even for a while in Europe.

Almost all the ecclesiastical princes from this dynasty had a passion for building, and influenced the planning not only through the grandiosity of their pretensions, sometimes bordering on hubris, but also creatively with

their own »inventions« and their astonishing profes-
sional knowledge. Principal among them was Prince-
Bishop Johann Philipp Franz von Schönborn, founder of
the Würzburg Residence, with no less than four brothers
and three cousins who were ecclesiastical dignitaries,
among them his successor in Würzburg, Friedrich Carl
von Schönborn, who was Imperial Vice-Chancellor in
Vienna, and his uncle Lothar Franz von Schönborn, who
was Elector of Mainz and Arch-Chancellor of the Empire.
The Würzburg Residence, on which the patronage of this
extraordinary family was concentrated, is the magnificent result of this Schönborn passion.

*View across the
garden to the
south façade of
the Residence*

8

# History

The prince-bishops of Würzburg resided in the fortress of Marienberg (on the hill above the town) until the beginning of the 18th century. It was not until the reign of Johann Philipp Franz von Schönborn (1719–1724) that the court was transferred to the town below. However, the modest little palace erected on the site of the present Residence was quite inadequate for the requirements of the Prince-Bishop, who had been nurtured in the traditions of absolutism and had very decided views as to what befitted his princely rank. When, in the very first year of his reign, he obtained what was for those days the vast sum of 600,000 florins through a lawsuit, he was able to give full rein to his passion for building. He ordered his court architect, Balthasar Neumann, to prepare plans for an extensive new Residence without delay. The plans were delivered not long after, and at least in the same year. The Prince-Bishop's relatives – his uncle Lothar Franz von Schönborn, Elector of Mainz, and his brother Friedrich Carl in Vienna, took advantage of this unique opportunity to build »castles in the air«, and in the temperamental and self-willed manner of the family at once intervened in the planning. The Elector of Mainz was advised by his court architect, Maximilian von Welsch, as well as by Johann Dientzenhofer, the creator of his summer residence at Pommersfelden, and a host of gentlemen-architects, while the Vienna Vice-Chancellor brought in Lucas von Hildebrandt, at that time the leading architect in the imperial capital. Balthasar Neumann's original ground-plan was the basis of all further planning. At the suggestion of Maximilian

*Prince-Bishop Johann Philipp Franz von Schönborn (1719–1724) who initiated the building of the Residence (section from the portrait in the Princes' Hall, Room 42)*

von Welsch, the number of courtyards enclosed within the lateral blocks was doubled and the façades on both sides were accentuated not by rectangular central pavilions but by convexly projecting transverse oval ones. The proposals of Lucas von Hildebrandt and the two French architects, Robert de Cotte and Germain Boffrand, mainly involved the façades. There were violent differences of opinion about the cour d'honneur be-

*The Würzburg Residence seen from the west, engraving by J. B. Gutwein from a drawing by M.A. Müller, 1757 (section)*

tween the protagonists of French château architecture on the one hand and of Viennese imperial baroque on the other, but Hildebrandt finally had his way. The decorative genius of this great Viennese architect is most in evidence in the central pavilion of the garden façade (Imperial Pavilion [Kaiserpavillon]). Reverting to the ideas of Johann Dientzenhofer, Balthasar Neumann nevertheless gave this most typically »Hildebrandt« section of

11

the Würzburg Residence a quite different function within the structure of the garden façade from that of the very similar centre block designed by the imperial architect for the Belvedere in Vienna. In fact Lucas von Hildebrandt had little or no influence on the ground-plan of the Würzburg Residence, but the magnificent gates of the cour d'honneur (demolished in 1821) certainly bear his mark. It is doubtful whether the rather strange façade system with two mezzanines, more characteristic of a town palais than a court residence, can be attributed to Hildebrandt. This feature is found nowhere else in his œuvre. It is equally alien to the work of the French architects, who in any case strongly opposed it, for the many small windows were a bourgeois rather than a courtly element. In fact the model for this system was created by Jacob van Campen with the town hall in Amsterdam; this in turn, as was the case with the Munich Residence, was one of the variations of the façade system developed in northern Italy, above all in Genoa. In Würzburg, however, the overall effect differs in that the ground floor and mezzanine look like a single storey because of the embossment, which reinforces the separation from the piano nobile. The mezzanine may well have been introduced into the plans by the Prince-Bishop and his architects because the limited dimensions of the site precluded any further extension of the ground-plan.

The two gifted rivals, Balthasar Neumann and Lucas von Hildebrandt, clashed in particular over the plans for the

*Giovanni Battista Tiepolo and his son Domenico, detail from the staircase fresco*

Würzburg Court Chapel. In the end, Balthasar Neumann's brilliant polyphonic spatial concept prevailed, and only the decoration was Hildebrandt's work. Architectural planning in the baroque era was in any case generally collective – quite apart from the constant interference by the patrons and gentlemen-architects. Most of the great palaces were the result of a joint effort. In the case of Würzburg, no single architect, not even Balthasar Neumann, had absolute authority. But, as his preliminary plans show, his role was not merely passive and conciliative; from the very beginning he took an active, creative part in the planning. Although he had to make concessions, first to Maximilian von Welsch, then to the French, and above all to Lucas von Hildebrandt, he always managed to regain the initiative. He continued to defend the fundamental idea of his original plan – the earliest one we have of the Würzburg Residence – and eventually succeeded in carrying it out, albeit with considerable alterations, against all opposition. The fact that the Würzburg Residence is not merely a conglomeration of disparate concepts or a reproduction of Viennese or French château architecture, but rather a work of art in its own right, the origin of Würzburg rococo, is due to the joint achievement of the Würzburg court architect, Balthasar Neumann, and his stubborn but none the less magnanimous patrons, Johann Philipp Franz von Schönborn and his brother Friedrich Carl. The Prince-Bishop was quick to recognize the outstanding talent of Balthasar Neumann, otherwise

*Balthasar Neumann, detail from the staircase fresco*

13

he would hardly have entrusted the coordination of one of the greatest building enterprises of the day to an almost unknown architect. Although Balthasar Neumann was already 32 years old, he had only just completed his training, having arrived at architecture only after a considerable detour. It can nonetheless be assumed that he had already proved himself, and this is also evident from his preliminary plan. Its distinctive feature is the combination of contrasting types of palace architecture. By connecting two self-contained four-winged buildings with inner courtyards by a transverse block, he created a specifically baroque, horseshoe-shaped complex with an open cour d'honneur, which differed from the usual three-winged complex in that the lateral blocks enclosed inner courtyards. The charm of this simple but nonetheless brilliant concept lies in the variety of its aspects: the palace looks different from every side, being, to some extent a complex of various types of palace. The accents also shift continually. On the side facing the town, for instance, although the emphasis is on the entrance to the cour d'honneur, this in no way includes the square as a whole. Viewed diagonally, on the other hand, the accent shifts more to the two lateral blocks. The length of their façades is extended even further by the corner projections, while in the case of the side and garden façades, the central axis is both interrupted and emphasized by convexly projecting pavilions. Here Maximilian von Welsch's oval pavilions (long out-dated in France and already a somewhat regressive element in Viennese palace architecture) were merely a rhythmic enrichment and in fact rather obscured the basic idea developed so logically and consistently by Balthasar Neumann in his early project. It is interesting to note that in this first plan, Balthasar Neumann provided for a width of 167 metres, with almost the same number of axes as the version that was eventually constructed.

Leaving aside the preliminary planning phase, there were three different stages in the building of the Würzburg Residence. The first began with the laying of the foundation stone by Prince-Bishop Johann Philipp Franz von Schönborn on 22 May 1720, before the plans had even been quite finished. The Prince-Bishop, who was impatient for the building to be completed but died not very long after and was never to see it in its finished state, moved to the Rosenbachhof in the immediate vicinity of the Residence, in order to have the new building under his constant supervision. The northern block was begun first, but without the »Church in the Oval« envisaged by Maximilian von Welsch, as there was still some uncertainty about this. Instead priority was given to the north-west pavilion on the town side, and this was as good as finished by 1723. The façade system for the vast building would thus have been finally established, had it not been for a measure of uncertainty which emerged over the planning of the whole project. The ideas which had originated from Maximilian von Welsch had lost their attraction, not least because they had been superseded by developments in French château architecture. In view of this, the Prince-Bishop dispatched his court architect to Paris, which at that time was the haute école of palace architecture in the West. Balthasar Neumann had further orders to acquaint himself with the latest developments in interior decoration, which had also entered a completely new phase.

Robert de Cotte (1656–1735), whom Balthasar Neumann first consulted, noticed that the plans for Würzburg were in many respects Italianate, in particular the changes suggested by Maximilian von Welsch, who had been influenced by the first phase of the Viennese imperial baroque style under Fischer von Erlach. In the alterations to the plans which the arrogant de Cotte »offered without interest«, he eliminated the lateral ovals, including the »Church in the Oval«, as well as the mezzanine in the façade system, and he even sought to do away with the splendid »invention« of the Prince-Bishop himself, the two symmetrical staircases. Instead he contributed a magnificent gallery running the whole length of the southern lateral front.

The distinctive, almost academic nature of the French school of palace architecture is illustrated by the fact that the plans presented by the very different and above all far more accommodating Germain Boffrand, who himself visited Würzburg in 1724 to view the new building and was impressed by the plans, particularly for the staircase, basically differed very little from those of his colleague. It is more than probable that Balthasar Neumann welcomed many of the French proposals, above all those which helped to eliminate the alterations made by Maximilian von Welsch. At any rate, from then on there was no more talk of the »Church in the Oval«. Apart from the enfilade in the Imperial Apartments of the garden front, however, the French only succeeded in abolishing the mezzanines and the pediments on the projections and adding the balconies overlooking the cour d'honneur, without however giving the façades any of the coldness or pathos of the French style. Hildebrandt's light-hearted Viennese concept and his decorative, festive pediment motif in any case provided a counterbalance. Balthasar Neumann successfully defended the four projections in the cour d'honneur against de Cotte, thereby renewing the original emphasis in his design on the lateral blocks as four-winged complexes.

Needless to say, work had continued incessantly on the Residence while Balthasar Neumann was in Paris. No sooner had he returned with his new ideas, however, than his tireless, often ruthless patron suddenly died, so suddenly that poison was suspected. The death of the Prince-Bishop, who, as his uncle remarked, was »hated throughout the country«, was greeted with rejoicing. The opposition party rallied for the attack and elected the learned and modest Christoph Franz von Hutten (1724–1729) as his successor. Only the north block, which was still under construction – barely a fifth of the vast complex – had been roofed, and work on the rest of the Residence was discontinued. The members of the house of Schönborn, however, who viewed the erection of the Würzburg Residence as a matter of prestige affecting the whole family, had no intention of resigning themselves to the circumstances. The Elector of Mainz, Lothar Franz von Schönborn, protected Balthasar Neumann, who remained in charge of the building process. After the early death of Prince-Bishop Christoph Franz von Hutten only a few years later, he was succeeded as Prince-Bishop of Würzburg by the Imperial Vice-Chancellor Friedrich Carl von Schönborn (1729–1746), brother of Johann Philipp Franz. Once again a man of the world, highly educated and with considerable political influence was in office, and it was at this point that the third building phase began, which ended with the completion of the shell of the Residence. Construction was resumed with great enthusiasm, the only difference being that Balthasar Neumann, who was again in charge, now had to deal not with architects from Mainz and Paris but with Lucas von Hildebrandt, at that time the leading exponent of Viennese imperial baroque, whose work the new Prince-Bishop considered to be »the best architecture of the day«.

Since the Imperial Vice-Chancellor only made the final move to Würzburg in 1734, in 1730 Balthasar Neumann travelled to Vienna with new plans. Lucas von Hildebrandt, a difficult and extremely irritable character with whom Balthasar Neumann nevertheless hoped to be able

*Court Garden gate, wrought-iron work by Georg and Anton Oegg, 1745–1774*

to get on, visited Würzburg in 1731. Neither the Prince-Bishop nor his architects ever seriously considered implementing the outdated ideas from Mainz or Paris. Balthasar Neumann's 1730 plan thus substituted rectangular projections for the typically baroque ovals of Maximilian von Welsch. He sited the Court Chapel neither in the Northern Oval, as had been envisaged by Maximilian von Welsch, nor in the connecting wing of the north block, as Germain Boffrand had proposed, but in the south-west corner of the south block, where it was in fact later built, against the will not only of the Prince-Bishop but also of Neumann's rival, Lucas von Hildebrandt, who was only responsible for the decoration. The Garden Hall in its present form with its ring of columns supporting the vaulting was also planned at this stage.

Otherwise the plans concentrated on the façades of the cour d'honneur and the garden front. In 1730 work began first on the southern counterpart of the completed north block, and in 1732 proceeded with the front facing the cour d'honneur and the town wing. Rapid progress was made everywhere, and more was achieved in 1733 than in any previous year. There was a temporary hold-up in 1734, due to the War of the Polish Succession, but work on the corps de logis was resumed the next year. 1736 saw the completion of the southern half of the cour d'honneur and the garden front, and in 1737 the staircase was begun. In 1738 the corps de logis on the main floor was finished and work started on the roof over the White Hall, followed in 1739 by the staircase and the Imperial Hall. As soon as the garden front was finished in 1740, the decoration of the Imperial Apartments south of the Kaisersaal began. By 1741 the entire shell, with the exception of the northern oval, had been roofed over. In 1742 the great vaulted ceilings in the Imperial Hall and the White Hall were constructed, followed in 1743 by the ceiling of the staircase. In December 1744, 24 years after the laying of the foundation stone, the shell of the building was completed. A celebration of thanksgiving was held with 16 Masses. One year later, in 1745, Maximilian von Welsch and Lucas von Hildebrandt both died, followed in 1746 by the Prince-Bishop and patron. The fate of the Residence seemed at first to be sealed, for the next prince-bishop, the profit-seeking, avaricious Count Anselm Franz von Ingelheim, was solely interested in moneymaking. Balthasar Neumann fell out of favour and was dismissed, and the building deteriorated. This unhappy intermezzo however ended only three years later with the death in 1749 of this grasping prince of the church who was mourned by no one. He was succeeded by Carl Philipp von Greiffenklau, who, while not a member of the Schönborn family, shared their origins and gifts. He continued the tradition of princely patronage begun by the Schönborn family. In the first month of his reign he reinstated Balthasar Neumann in his old office; the architect now turned his attention to the design of the gardens and square and to the continuation of the interior decoration.

## HIGHLIGHTS OF THE INTERIOR

There are two highlights in the history of the interior decoration of the Würzburg Residence; the first occurring during the reign of Friedrich Carl von Schönborn (1729–1746, Second Episcopal Apartment, the Imperial Apartments and the Court Chapel); the second inspired by Carl Philipp von Greiffenklau (1749–1754, painting of the Imperial Hall and the staircase by Tiepolo). Classicism (the Ingelheim Rooms) and the Empire period (the »Tuscany Rooms«) however also left their mark on the Residence; in the Second World War, however, everything but the small amount of movable furnishing and art treasures which had been stored in a safe place was destroyed. The first rooms were already furnished under Prince-Bishop Christoph Franz von Hutten (1724–1729) in the north block, although he did not live to occupy this original Episcopal Apartment. Only a few traces of this suite of rooms, which were later redecorated in the neoclassical style (Ingelheim Rooms), have remained. Germain Boffrand designed the interior of this First Episcopal Apartment which was furnished relatively simply but entirely in the spirit of French art with a predominance of Regency forms. The sculptors Claude Curé and Jacob van der Auvera, the stuccoers Johann Peter and Karl Anton Castelli, the painter Anton Clemens Lünenschloß and the tapestry-weaver Andreas Pirot collaborated in this work. The interior decorations of the Würzburg Residence did not however attain international standards until the reign

of Friedrich Carl von Schönborn, who furnished the
Second Episcopal Apartment, this time in the south block,
the Court Chapel and some of the guest and imperial
rooms on the side facing the garden. It was no longer Paris
but the imperial capital of Vienna that was now the
dominant influence, although only during the first phase
until the death of the court painter and designer Rudolph
Byss, since the Viennese decorative art forms were by
then in many respects already out of date. In Würzburg,
however, the designers soon moved on from this phase.
It is highly unlikely that the change to rococo was influenced by Austria for Austria, unlike Würzburg, never developed its own variation of this style. It is not certain to
what extent the Würzburg development was stimulated by
the court art of the Wittelsbachs in Munich and by Bavarian rococo, as was for example the case in Ans-

21

bach. Members of the Guthmann family, woodcarvers who came from Munich, were certainly responsible for a remarkably large proportion of the decorations and furnishings in Würzburg. Balthasar Neumann in fact assembled a large number of gifted artists and craftsmen of varying origin: Italians, Germans, French and Dutch, who soon combined to form a creative team. From 1734/35 this included Antonio Bossi, probably the most outstanding stuccoer of his day, the sculptor Johann Wolfgang van der Auvera, the wood-carver and cabinet-maker Ferdinand Hund, the gifted court locksmith Johann Georg Oegg, who like the court potter and porcelainmaker Dominikus Eder came from Vienna, and the painters Anton Joseph Högler, Johann Thalhofer and Georg Anton Urlaub. The constant interchange of artistic ideas in this international group of artists produced an independent rococo form of remarkable individuality – Würzburg rococo, one of the richest and most exuberant of all the variations of this style in Germany. This brief but exquisite flowering of Franconian art produced some of the finest interiors in Germany and beyond, where styles and ideas from outside the country were combined with older local traditions.

The iconology of the Würzburg Residence is also a continuation of older traditions in German palace architecture, traditions founded during the Counter-Reformation, particularly in the electoral palaces in Munich and Aschaffenburg, but which also returned to older medieval concepts. This is reflected in the formal state rooms and guest apartments in many ways characteristic of palace architecture in the Catholic areas of Germany, the rooms which, as »imperial rooms« and »imperial halls«, were furnished and permanently kept ready for a visit by the emperor. In Würzburg as in Aschaffenburg, the Imperial Apartments had a real significance, as emperors stopped there regularly on their journey to Frankfurt for

the coronation ceremony. The Imperial Hall in Würzburg
– the name was recorded for the first time in 1754 and
dates back to long before this – is one of the last in a
long series of halls and rooms termed imperial and from
its artistic quality probably the most important. The iconography departs from the usual mythological representations in European palaces (the labours of Hercules, etc.),
and does not to any great extent depict the allegorical
world of absolutism, but rather reflects the medieval
history of the episcopal principality of Würzburg.
This is no doubt because the political existence of the
episcopal principality of Würzburg could be compre-
hended only within the context of the history of the Holy
Roman Empire, while the objective presence of this history was virtually absent from the new Residence building. In 1735 the Würzburg Jesuit Seyfried drafted an extensive iconographic programme (which is unlikely to
have been produced solely on his own initiative), designed to compensate for the historical element missing
in the new building. It bore the title »Preliminary Ob-
servations on How the Style of Painting in the New
Residence should be Conceived«, and had a decidedly
one-sided emphasis on state, political and historical
elements. The new Prince-Bishop, while accepting the
basic ideas, at the same time probably realized that pro-
grammes alone, no matter how learned and profound,
were inadequate if they were not reproduced with the appropriate artistic skill. It would seem that the ceiling of
the Garden Hall which Johann Zick from Lachen completed in 1750 was not entirely satisfactory, for the artist
departed the same year for Bruchsal, where he painted
the ceiling for Balthasar Neumann's staircase. Prince-
Bishop Carl Philipp von Greiffenklau clearly wanted
something better. After an unfortunate interlude with
the »devil« Joseph Visconti from Milan, for a princely sum the fresco genius Giovanni Battista Tiepolo

agreed to come to Würzburg. Tiepolo arrived with his two sons, the 23-year-old Domenico and the 14-year-old Lorenzo, in December 1750 and worked until July 1752 on three frescos in the Imperial Hall: »The wedding of Barbarossa and Beatrix of Burgundy« (which took place in Würzburg in 1156), »The granting of the Franconian title of duke by Barbarossa in 1168«, and, for the ceiling, »Apollo conducting Emperor Barbarossa's bride to him in the sun chariot«. In 1752–1753 he then produced the largest ceiling fresco ever painted for the enormous vault above staircase: »Homage to the Prince-Bishop as patron of the arts under the protection of the sun god Apollo«, with allegories of the four continents of the earth and portraits of the principal artists involved with the Residence. Tiepolo, who by then had already developed his uniquely luminous style to perfection and had reached the zenith of his creative power, had never before and never again painted rooms of such vast dimensions and dynamic conception. Here two great works of architecture and painting combine to form an unparalleled synthesis of the arts. Tiepolo left Würzburg on 8 November 1753, after almost three years' work. Balthasar Neumann had died shortly before, living long enough to see the painting of what had been the main work of his life. He was followed one year later by his last patron, Prince-Bishop Carl Philipp von Greiffenklau. The era of Würzburg rococo had come to an end.

## COMPLETION, DESTRUCTION AND RECONSTRUCTION

The reign of the Prince-Bishop of Würzburg and Bamberg, Adam Friedrich von Seinsheim (1755–1779) brought to the Residence the noble but somewhat austere art of the Louis-Seize era. Ludovico Bossi produced neoclassical stucco decoration for the staircase in

1765/66, and Franz Anton Ermeltraut added neoclassical grisaille paintings to the vestibule. While work was still in progress on the last state apartments on the garden side as well as on the Princes' Hall, the Ingelheim rooms were already being decorated for the second time, this time in early neoclassical style. The Court Gardens were completed and finally the official architect Geigel provided a solution for integrating the complex into the architecture of the town which reflected the lack of creative impulse at this period. Balthasar Neumann had conceived the square in front of the Residence as a grandiose »calotte« stage on which the many different aspects of the vast building would appear, so to speak, in various acts, both in sequence and in unison. Geigel gave firm contours to the square by placing a building on each side. To balance the Rosenbachhof, he placed a replica, the Ambassadorial Building, on the opposite, south side, extending both buildings by adding arcades terminating in high columns (obelisks).

With the advent of secularization, the episcopal principality of Würzburg was abolished. In 1802 the bishopric was transferred for the first time to Bavaria. It was not however permanently incorporated into Bavaria until 1814, after the eight-year interregnum of the Grand Duke Ferdinand III of Tuscany, under whom the Episcopal Apartment was redecorated in Empire style from designs by the Frenchman Alexandre Salins de Montfort. By this time there was so little understanding for the concept of the enormous building (due to the influence of neoclassicism and Prince-Bishop Erthal) that Joh. G. Oegg's gates, which curved gracefully across the cour d'honneur and projected into the square outside, were demolished in 1821. They were far more than a mere ornamental feature – they were, in some respects, the key to the interpretation of this dynamic complex of buildings. The external appearance of the Würzburg Residence has been radically altered by the removal of these gates, and the front now »gapes«.

In the course of the 19th century, Crown Prince Ludwig and various kings of Bavaria resided in the Würzburg palace, if only for brief periods. The Prince Regent Luitpold was born in the Tuscany suite in 1821. In the 1920s, work began on the restoration of the decoration and furnishings of the interiors, which proceeded according to strict preservation principles and was aimed at recreating the original historical state. Then, on 16 March 1945, disaster struck when a heavy air raid with incendiary bombs destroyed most of the town and with it the

Residence, of which only the outer shell was left intact. Only the corps de logis with Balthasar Neumann's magnificent sequence of rooms and the paintings of Tiepolo survived the inferno. This was largely due to the technical genius of Balthasar Neumann who, against the advice of Lucas von Hildebrandt, risked spanning the immense spaces in the vestibule, staircase and Imperial Hall with unsupported stone ceilings. This vaulting withstood the fires of 1896 and 1945 and is still intact today. The Bavarian Palace Department at once took steps to repair the immediate damage and secure what was left. But the fact that Tiepolo's frescos were not destroyed by damp was primarily due to John D. Skilton, the American officer responsible for the protection of art treasures, who promptly obtained the necessary slates and wood for the provisional roofing. By 1950 the corps de logis had largely been restored. The last topping out ceremony was held in 1959, but for structural reasons new and difficult operations had to be undertaken between 1964 and 1966 to ensure the safety of the building. The corps de logis was provided with a supporting steel casing, and the twin columns between the vestibule and the staircase were replaced by massive supporting pillars.

Meanwhile, since a new use had to be found for large sections of the Residence, various state institutions were now housed here (Würzburg University, the Martin von Wagner Museum, the state archives and the offices of the state vineyards, etc.)

Nevertheless, the work of restoration proceeded apace. One of the greatest achievements was the restoration of the Court Chapel, which was reopened to the public in May 1963. The reconstruction of the Tuscany Hall in the university section was completed in 1965. The difficult, laborious restoration and partial renewal of the great state apartments was also commenced. This was pos-

sible because the movable furnishings and considerable sections of the wall panels had been removed and stored during the war, thus escaping destruction. The Southern Imperial Apartments were completed in May 1970 and their northern counterparts in December 1974. The Ingelheim Rooms and the Princes' Hall were reopened in September 1978. In 1981, the Würzburg Residence, including the square in front of it (Residenzplatz) and the Court Gardens, was included in UNESCO's »World Cultural Heritage List« and placed under special protection. Reconstruction of the Mirror Cabinet in the Southern Imperial Apartments was completed in October 1987.

*The war-damaged Residence with the first new roofs, as it looked in 1947*

# Court Gardens

Although the history of the Court Gardens is as old as that of the Residence itself, it was only in the reign of Prince-Bishop Adam Friedrich von Seinsheim (1755–1779), when the palace was basically complete both outside and inside, that the project progressed beyond the stage of preliminary planning. The plans were conditioned by the architecture of the palace and the nature of the terrain. The main limitation was the fact that this was not a summer residence but a town palace that was still within the walls, though on the periphery of the town. As the possibility of making a breach in these walls was never seriously considered, the space available for the usual palace gardens was limited from the start. There was only room to the east and south of the Residence. And as the Residence is a complex of many different types of palace architecture, so the Court Gardens are not symmetrical and uniform in style but consist rather of several virtually independent sectors which spread out in different directions from the south and east fronts of the Residence and are combined into a loose artistic unit only by the architecture of the palace itself. The total area of the gardens, however, is little more than three times that of the Residence. A classical French lay-out with canals and avenues stretching away to the horizon was, therefore, out of the question from the start. The Residence and its gardens not only had to respect the existing bastions, they had to incorporate them. The Residence is in fact located at the base of the regular but stilted triangle formed by the bastion, so that its main architectural axis coincides with the apex of the triangle

*View of the flowerbeds framing the South Garden*

and is directed towards the tip of the bastion. The governing factor was thus not the architecture of the palace but the bastion! The extended main axis of the Residence is capped by the bastion and the space is thus dominated by the architectonic energies of the bastion, not the Residence. The layout of the gardens had even less in common with the French style in that the terrain between the Residence and the fortifications was not flat and even, but rose in three terraces to the height of the rampart, from which a waterfall was designed to cascade. It was not the extended architectural axis of the Residence but the splendid amphitheatre provided by the bastion which determined the layout of the east garden section. This more intimate portion of the gardens was clearly influenced by Italian rather than French traditions, as well as earlier forms of German garden design going right back to Furttenbach.

The situation was rather different in the gardens in front of the southern lateral façade of the Residence. The layout of this section was determined by the Residence alone and not by the existence of a bastion but. The parterre is separated from the southern lateral front and bounded on the opposite side by the orangery. It consists of a rectangle subdivided in the style of Austrian gardens by paths running along the main axes and diagonals, with a circular pool in the centre. Here however, the main axis, which is an extension of the oval projection of the façade, is noticeably the least developed, the path being not only narrower than all the others but in addition obscured by two groups of statuary. The main emphasis is on the path which cuts across the rectangle, dividing it into two unequal halves and thereby bending the diagonals and making them less important. This path runs parallel to the south façade, meeting the avenue running from north to south, which is the real main axis of the whole garden complex: it functions, as it were, as the

hinge between the two sections of the garden, each of which opens out in a different direction, the first one to the east, the second one to the west. It was not the axis leading from front to back, as in French garden design, but rather the transverse axis, as is found in many German gardens, that was important here. Projecting from the south-east corner of the Residence is a garden that serves to link the two main sections and thus, with good reason, mostly contained a maze. Adjoining this feature was the open-air theatre found in almost all great German gardens.

*Design for the East Garden by the court gardener Johann Prokop Mayer*

This concept of the gardens, which in many respects was governed by the architecture of the Residence and the nature of the terrain, was maintained from the 1720s through all four stages of development until its final implementation in the 1770s, with only the details altered as was appropriate.

In the earliest plans dating from 1722/23, the east garden appears either as a level space with six pools or already as a terraced garden with a cascade; both versions provided for an orangery at the end of the extended main axis. At this stage the design of the south garden was strictly symmetrical, with four formal beds surrounding a central pool. The south-east section linking the two main gardens was to have a gallery of lime trees and an open-air theatre. Maximilian von Welsch's designs show richly structured but somewhat schematically arranged formal flower beds. The extended main axis in front of the Imperial Pavilion is not opened up by paths but is for good reason concealed by formal beds.

An interesting innovation in garden planning, which certainly far surpassed the concepts current in Italian and French garden design at the time, was introduced by Balthasar Neumann's plan of 1730, which for the first time incorporated the summit of the rampart in the layout. On top of the rampart, with access via a system of terraces, ramps and steps, he planned a promenade on the boundary between the gardens and the open countryside. This promenade was to encircle the two bastions in front of the south and east gardens and provide a view, as from a balcony, over the gardens on the one side and the countryside on the other. An essential feature of the English landscape garden, the encircling path or belt, thus makes its appearance here, in an otherwise strictly geometrical concept, at a surprisingly early date, although by no means for the first time on the Continent (cf. the Hermitage at Bayreuth).

In a series of plans developed in 1738, Balthasar Neu-mann replaced the Austrian-style schematic articulation of the south garden by a parterre of subtle construction with rich formal beds, connecting it more effectively with the east garden through the use of lateral sections. The court gardener Johann Demeter finally laid out the south garden in 1756–1758 according to the plans of the architect and captain Johann Michael Fischer, a pupil of Balthasar Neumann. In addition, in 1759 the Bavarian court architect François Cuvilliés the Elder worked on

*View of the East Garden with the steps, ramps and terrace walls on either side*

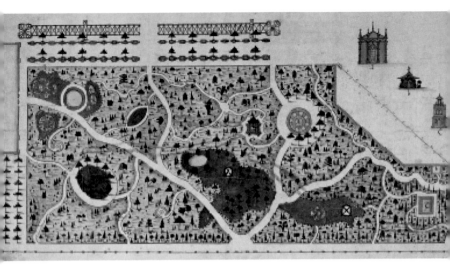

*Geigel's design for the landscape garden section in the southwest part of the Court Gardens*

the model for the grand flight of steps and in 1767 Balthasar Neumann's son was also involved. The Seven Years' War however held up the work to such an extent that on Demeter's death in 1769 the south garden was still unfinished and the east garden not even begun. Real progress only began when Adam Friedrich von Seinsheim summoned Johann Prokop Mayer, a native of Bohemia, to Würzburg in 1770 and appointed him court gardener. Mayer, who had learnt his craft in France and had recently been employed in England, showed remarkable appreciation of the situation, and designed for Würzburg (»one of the most beautiful palaces in Europe«) not an English landscape garden but a symmetrical geometric complex which surpassed everything hitherto planned or completed, while in no way abandoning the original concept. On a similar principle to Balthasar Neumann's sequence of rooms, he conceived an enfilade of »garden rooms« which intersected and interlocked to form a complex whole. In front of the Imperial

Pavilion was a circular sunken parterre with fountains, which extended into the second terrace and was laid out with radial and bell-shaped sections and formal beds. On the second terrace, which was reached by ramps and peripheral pergolas, was a small, intimate cabinet garden (Princes' Garden) with a pool and cascade. Flights of steps on either side of the garden led from here up to the ramparts. Mayer employed all the devices of centuries of garden tradition, and with its spatial contrasts and intersections this small but sophisticated complex of gardens was unique in Germany in its day.

By contrast with the terraced east garden, the south garden formed a rectangular »garden hall«. It was extended to the west by a hedge garden and a further axis was added, angled towards the tip of the second bastion. The remarkable classicistic garden statues, mostly of Savoyard boys, Chinese, Moorish children, vases and cartouches, as well as »The abduction of Europa« and »The abduction of Proserpina« on the central axis of the south garden, are the work of Johann Peter Wagner and his atelier (the originals were all replaced by copies at the beginning of the 20th century). This section is bounded on the south side by an orangery built as a hothouse in 1756–1758. The rococo wrought-iron gates at the entrance from the court promenade, completed by Joh. G. Oegg in 1748–1751, are a generation older. Also dating from this period are the wrought-iron gates with the arms of Prince-Bishop Anselm Franz von Ingelheim, which were additionally crowned with the monogram of Prince-Bishop Adam Friedrich von Seinsheim in 1764/65.

When the latter died in 1778, the gardens were still not quite finished. In the meantime garden design had progressed far beyond the creations of Johann Prokop Mayer. The Court Gardens at Würzburg were now outdated with the advent of the English landscape garden, which had revolutionized garden design throughout Europe. Prince-Bishop Franz Ludwig von Erthal (1779–1799), who, like his brother Friedrich Carl, Elector and Archbishop of Mainz, was an adherent of the English landscape garden, rejected the old geometrical style of the Court Gardens as »affected and contrived«. The cascade planned for the east garden was thus never built and the area south of the Residence Square (Residenzplatz) was converted in 1793 by Amtmann Geigel into a landscape garden. After a long period in the 19th century when the gardens were looked after exactly as they were, a moderate programme of renovation based on the principles of preservation has been introduced over the last few decades. This has included making the magnificent amphitheatre with its elaborate structure in the east garden visible again by clearing away the trees and shrubs that had grown in profusion around it.

*Section from a plan of the Würzburg Court Gardens dating from 1803. To the right of the the two orangery wings are the grounds of the St Afra Monastery, surrounded by a wall*

## THE KITCHEN GARDEN
## SOUTH OF THE ORANGERY

In the 17th and 18th centuries, ornamental principles were applied to numerous court kitchen gardens, and they were displayed with pride as gardens in their own right. At the beginning of the 19th century, a kitchen garden of this type was also laid out in the Court Gardens of the Würzburg Residence. It was located south of the orangery and occupied an area of approximately 5,000 m² which had recently been separated from the neighbouring monastery of St Afra and surrounded by a wall. The outstanding features of this kitchen garden at the edge of the Court Gardens were the artistically clipped fruit trees and espaliers. The original design with an almost right-angled grid of paths and ten vegetable beds of similar size remained almost unchanged until the 1960s. The central and transverse paths were lined with

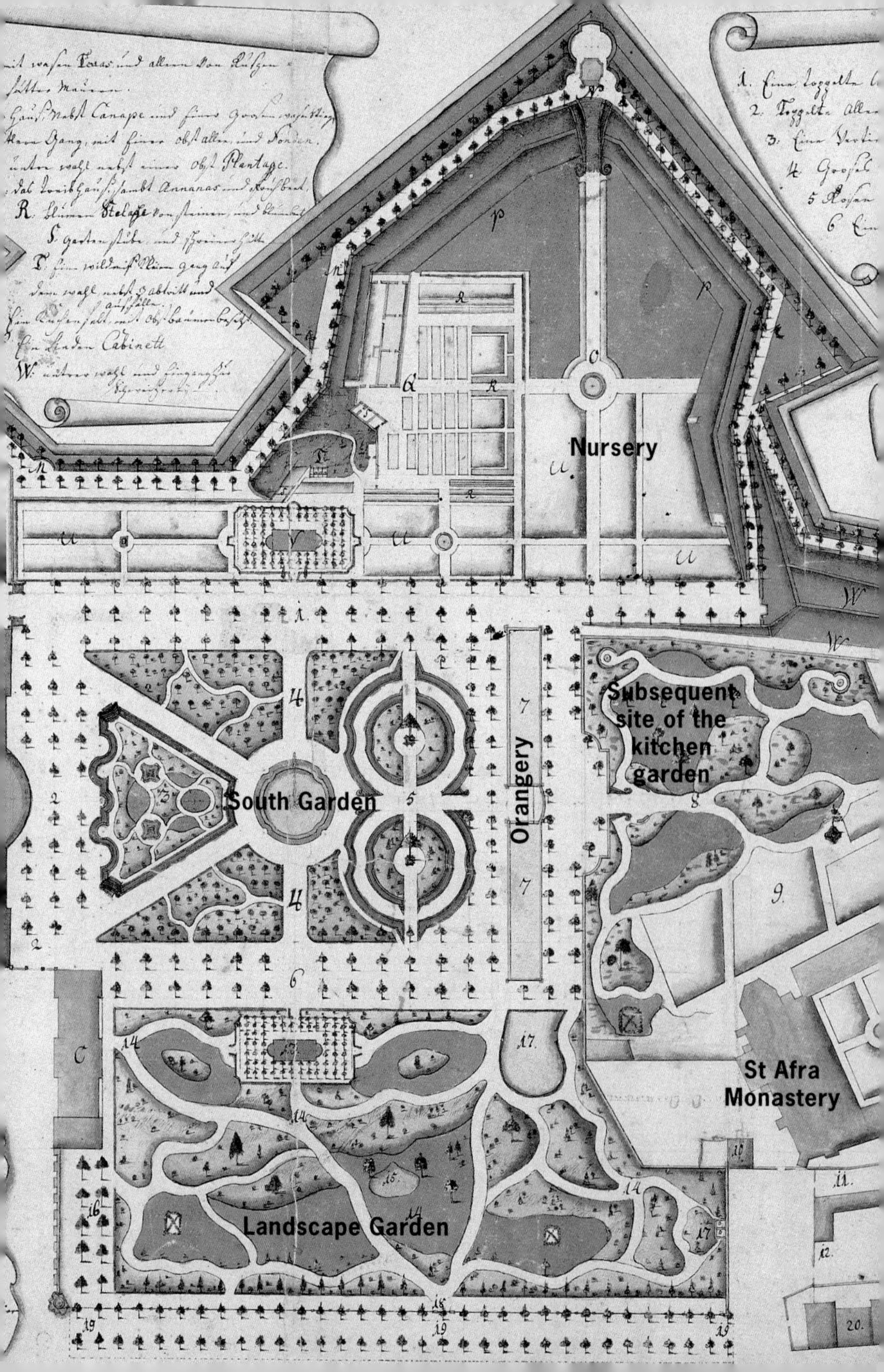

Nursery

Subsequent site of the kitchen garden

South Garden

Orangery

St Afra Monastery

Landscape Garden

tall fruit trees, pruned to form alternating conical and open funnel shapes. These elaborate forms have been almost entirely forgotten, but were widespread in gardens at the end of the 18th century. The fruit that ripened on the crowns of these trees was of excellent quality and was served to the court as dessert fruit. In the course of the 20th century the cultivation of useful plants gradually became less important and finally ceased in 1969. After the fruit trees had been felled and the old vegetable beds levelled, they were replaced by a simple lawn with a path around it and a row of lime trees along the wall of the neigh-

*The orangery with the kitchen garden in front of it*

*Right: Section from the original cadastral plan with the south part of the Court Gardens, 1837*

bouring Kilianeum. In front of the terrace wall of the orangery and the western enclosing wall there was a bed with perennials and shrubs, and a few seats. In 1997 the Bavarian Palace Department decided to recreate the kitchen garden with its original structure of beds and paths and to plant it with historical and modern varieties of fruit and vegetables. The reconstruction of the kitchen garden took place in three stages from October 1998 to September 2001. Over 120 tall fruit trees and just under 60 berry-bearing shrubs were planted. In the next few years the crowns of the fruit trees will be shaped as they were at the beginning of the 19th century, and visitors to the Würzburg Court Gardens will once again be able to admire the horticultural art of fruit-tree clipping.

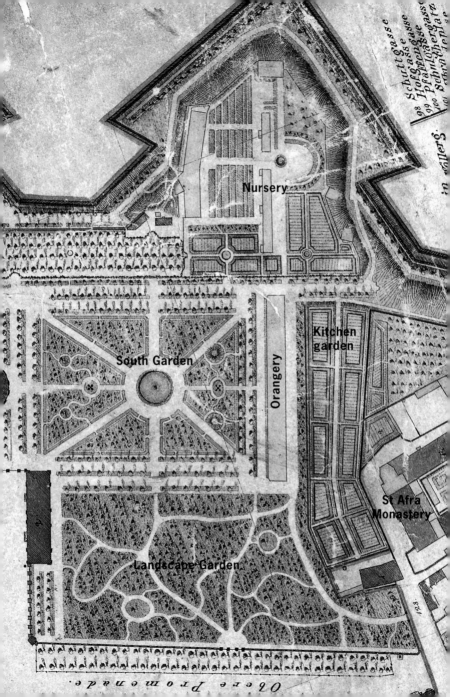

Nursery

South Garden

Orangery

Kitchen garden

Landscape Garden

St Afra Monastery

*Obere Promenade.*

98 Schützgasse
99 Holzgasse
100 Pfahlgasse
100 Schmidtergasse
101 Schrannenplatz

in Wällers

# The Residence Square and Front

The Residence seems in some ways too magnificent by German standards for the town. A great square, almost oppressively vast and – although not originally intended to be – empty, sets the Residence apart like a mountain from the huddle of buildings that is the old town. However, the architecture of the palace and the immense space of the square are in many ways dynamically related. The fact that the square slopes upwards towards the centre, curving convexly like a calotte stage, is an important element in this; as a result, the palace takes on a variety of aspects as the accent shifts. Moreover, the Residence is itself an unusual collection of very different and even contrary types of palace architecture combined to form a whole which is not however always harmonious. The result of this combination is a complex of open and enclosed blocks and wings, the façades of which vary in minor but nonetheless noticeable ways. The accents shift constantly. The gigantic structure has not one but many different aspects. At first sight it is dominated by the two blocks on either side, the fronts of which separate and continue around the corner as the side façades, while the cour d'honneur with the corps de logis disappears, so to speak, behind the horizon of the calotte stage. Then the massive building opens up to disclose a smaller space, the enclosed area of the cour d'honneur, which was originally separated from the square by the beautiful ornamental gates made by Joh. G. Oegg from a design by Lucas von Hildebrandt (demolished in 1821). While the visitor is brought close to the architecture of the palace in the cour d'honneur, this more intimate

*» . . . no palace in the whole of Germany can compare with this one.«*

Lothar Franz von Schönborn

*The central projection in the cour d'honneur behind the Franconia Fountain by Ferdinand v. Miller, 1894*

enclosure was at the same time linked with the spacious square outside by the filigree work of what were surely the most magnificent wrought-iron gates ever designed or made. The garden front and the side façades belong to other traditions and therefore relate in a different way to their surroundings.

The façade has four storeys, a ground and a main floor with mezzanines above each. However, because of the embossment the two lower storeys look like a single bottom floor, which in turn has the effect of raising the main storey. This system is not, however, consistent, since although the lateral blocks have four storeys, these are successively reduced as the cour d'honneur is approached. Although the lateral projections of the cour d'honneur still have four storeys, the lower mezzanine is virtually eliminated through the addition of a balcony. The corner pavilions only have pediments on their town side, while the side facing the cour d'honneur has merely a horizontal attic. As a result, the towering impression of these corner pavilions on the town side is reversed on

the cour d'honneur side, where the focus is more on the projecting balcony lower down, which is supported by solid Doric columns. This makes the side façades look rather forbidding by contrast with the festive aspect of the main façade. On the cour d'honneur side the lateral blocks have only three storeys, since the lower mezzanine has finally been omitted, but to compensate for this the ground floor is provided with gallery windows. Both mezzanines have disappeared from the main façade of the cour d'honneur, so that only the main floors remain. As a result – measured by human proportions – it appears more monumental, but compared with all the other façades it looks lower. The building complex dips in the centre, despite the immense decorative pediment above the central projection. Moreover, the »instrumentation« of the whole has a very festive character, from the pilasters on the lateral blocks to the half-columns of the cour d'honneur façade and the pathos of the full columns under the balconies of the ground floor. The reduction of the storeys to two floors can undoubtedly

*The west façade of the Residence has a total width of 168 m*

be attributed to French influence, whereas the large ornamental pediment is a characteristic feature of Lucas von Hildebrandt: two lions support the coat of arms of the patron, Prince-Bishop Friedrich Carl von Schönborn, surmounted by the imperial crown, which he was entitled to include as Bishop of both Würzburg and Bamberg. The coat of arms in the cartouches above the windows also has the imperial crown, and it is only missing in those of the north block, which was begun earlier. The cartouches above the central doorways of the side blocks were filled in the 19th century with the initials MJ (for King Max I Joseph of Bavaria). The triangular pediments of the side blocks feature allegories of Justice and Peace (north block) and of Harmony and Piety (south block). The façades would be perfectly symmetrical if it were not for the element of tension and irregularity introduced by the portal to the Court Chapel in the south block. Nearly all the sculptures are by Johann Wolfgang van der Auvera and his atelier and by Claude Curé; the wrought-iron gates in the north block were created by J. M. Lintz in 1728, and those in the south block by Johann Georg Oegg.

The façades did not incidentally originally show the stonework but were painted with stonewash. The structural parts and architectural articulations were silver grey against a yellow ochre background, while the attic sculptures were white. The proportions of this immense complex of buildings can be measured by the two smaller identical palaces on either side of the Residence, with arcades ending with high columns thrust forward like sentries and securing the sides of the great square. The Rosenbachhof on the left (on its pediment the allied arms of the Rosenbach and Stadion families) was built before the Residence from designs by Antonio Petrini in around 1700. Its counterpart, the Ambassadorial Building opposite, was not built until 1767, under the direction of

Amtmann Geigel, who also designed the arcades and high columns. The classicist sculptures are by Johann Peter Wagner; the fine wrought-iron work in the arcades are the creation of Georg Oegg, as are also the two wrought-iron gateways resembling triumphal arches flanking the town side of the Residence, to the south the Court Garden gate (Hofgartentor) and to the north the Rennweg gate. Both feature the monogram of the Würzburg Prince-Bishop Adam Friedrich von Seinsheim (1755–1779) with the imperial crown in the centre, while the side sections of the Rennweg gates display the monogram of Prince-Bishop Carl Philipp von Greiffenklau (1749–1754) and those of the Court Garden gates the initials of Prince-Bishop Anselm Franz von Ingelheim (1746–1749).

*Residence Square (Residenzplatz) with arcades and high columns, woodcut by Sebastian Roland, Nuremberg 1778*

# Halls in the central block

## ◼1◼ VESTIBULE

The dominant characteristic of this room is the contrast between its unusual breadth and the disproportionately low elevation of the vaulting, which is limited by the White Hall above. The vault, where the ribs are only in stucco-work, has been executed with remarkable technical skill: it is alarmingly shallow and spans the area without any upward impetus so that the ceiling is well-nigh horizontal – all this so that a coach could turn without difficulty in the spacious, unsupported hall. The neoclassical decoration added later however detracts considerably from the spatial impact of the vestibule. The stucco-work was created by Lodovico Bossi in 1765/66 and the trompe l'œil grisaille paintings are by Franz Anton Ermeltraut (view into a dome, with the labours of Hercules depicted in the drum). The niches on the south wall contain marble statues of Minerva and Bellona produced by Johann Peter Wagner in 1779. Only the atlantes carved out of the bosses by Johann Wolfgang van der Auvera in 1749 are contemporary with the building.

The vestibule was incidentally much better lit as long as Joh. G. Oegg's fanlight screen and wrought-iron gates to the Garden Hall, dating from 1749/50, were still in existence. In 1964–1965 the double columns between the vestibule and the staircase had to be replaced by massive pillars for structural reasons. The rather oppressively low proportions of the vestibule were no doubt also intended to provide an architectural contrast to the lofty staircase.

*View of the staircase from the vestibule (prior to the reinforcement of the double columns in 1964/65)*

*Garden Hall with ceiling fresco by Johann Zick, 1750*

## 2 GARDEN HALL (GARTENSAAL)

The Garden Hall is a wide room based on a transverse oval ground-plan. For its size it is disproportionately low, yet it nevertheless gives an impression of graceful lightness. This is not due to the proportions, which differ very little from those of the vestibule, nor to the ceiling frescos, which, though they open up the low vault with a vision of the celestial sphere, create a rather heavy impression with their earth-brown colours, but rather to the brilliant structure created by Balthasar Neumann. The vault is supported not by the walls alone but also by a ring of fine perpendicular columns. With cube-shaped pedestals and ceiling sections they stand freely in the light-filled room like figures in a round-dance. The

*Diana in repose, detail from the ceiling fresco by Johann Zick in the Garden Hall*

vaulting rises effortlessly from each one like the jet of a fountain. As a result the vault stands out from the walls like a baldachin. This type of room is more usually to be found in sacred than palace architecture.

The colours used in the room are light and cool. The stucco decoration created by Antonio Bossi in 1749, with light-blue motifs on a white background, pierced by sparkling fragments of mirror, are full of charm and still retain the lightness of his mature work. The stucco figures added a decade later however already signal the waning of his creative powers. Only the ceiling, painted by Johann Zick from Memmingen in 1750, introduces an element of solemnity and heaviness into this light room. The paintings depict »The banquet of the gods« and »Diana in repose«; the ring of columns is decorated with putti scenes.

## ▣ STAIRCASE (TREPPENHAUS)

*Staircase,
view from the
landing*

Architecture and painting have combined to make the
staircase at Würzburg one of the most magnificent tri-
umphs of secular building. The original plan envisaged
two relatively small staircases in the conventional horse-
shoe shape, one on each side of the vestibule. The design was then extended to provide for three flights of
stairs with landings, similar to the staircase finally constructed. Robert de Cotte finally eliminated one of the
two staircases which were the »invention« of the first
patron, and instead enlarged the other into a monumental
affair with five bays and a gallery. From then on Balthasar Neumann never lost sight of the idea of a gallery
on the upper storey. He went even further: he eliminated
the supporting cornice from the upper storey and
spanned the whole great five-bayed staircase with a single unsupported vault. The result was a construction of
magnificent spaciousness which even by French standards was »most impressive« (Germain Boffrand). In
1737 »the whole staircase« was completed, and by 1743
the vault was finished. According to a story told by
Balthasar Neumann's son about his father's rival, Lucas
von Hildebrandt, the great Viennese architect declared
that he would »have himself hanged at his own expense«
under the vault if it should hold, whereupon Balthasar
Neumann countered by offering to have a battery of artillery fired off under it. At any event the vault withstood
the disastrous air-raid in March 1945.
Originally the walls of the stairwell were not solid
around the first landing but opened up by arcades
through which light was admitted from the courtyard.
The staircase complex was set like a scaffold with five
bays with the light falling through it in the midst of the
vast hall; a complicated, lively display of flights and
counter-flights, rising and falling balustrades, terraced

landings and connecting galleries, which changed constantly and looked different from every stair. Instead of the rather pedantically ordered balusters of the classicistic balustrade, the original plans envisaged either a filigree construction by Oegg or a stone parapet by Johann Wolfgang van der Auvera or Ferdinand Tietz, which with its fragmented rocaille work would have swung lightly upwards. Instead of the arid classicistic stucco-work of Ludovico Bossi, (1765/66) one has to imagine Antonio Bossi's exuberant rococo decorations. The allegorical and mythological figures now on the balustrade were created by Johann Peter Wagner between 1771 and 1776; on the lower landing the four seasons, on the eastern flight Apollo and Paris as representatives of music, matched on the western flight by Meleager and Atalanta from the realm of hunting. On the shorter sides of the gallery on the upper floor are the hours of the day, and on the long sides further – but not very clearly defined – allegorical subjects.

*Two sculptures on the stair balustrade: Spring...*

Aside from its vast proportions, the extraordinary effect created by this staircase does not wholly depend either on the contrast between the crypt-like gloom of the vestibule and the radiant lightness of the upper gallery, or that between the forest of columns in the lower floor with its five bays and the liberating breadth of the unsupported upper floor spanned by a single great vault, but largely on the rapid, breathtaking sweep up from the oppressively low ceiling of the vestibule to the tremendous height of the vaulting above the stairs. What the visitor feels is a thrill of joy. Since when climbing the stairs between the walls of the stairwell he cannot see the confining walls on the sides, the vaulting seems to lose itself in infinite space and he is confronted with a whirling sea of light and colour.

It was Giovanni Battista Tiepolo who first contrived a fitting decoration for Balthasar Neumann's vault, filling the vast area measuring 30 x 18 metres with a single painting, the largest fresco ever produced. (Originally five small fields were planned). The programme of his composition included several complexes of traditional iconographical themes. The sun god Apollo predominated, not so much in the role of the allegorical deity of absolutism but as patron of the arts, together with the glorification of the Prince-Bishop as Franconian Maecenas, and his artists, whose fame is proclaimed by the four continents of the earth. The huge painting cannot be grasped all at once but as a sequence of separate themes. There are two central points in the composition.

First to be revealed, from the landing at the top of the lower centre flight of stairs, is the northern half of the painting. At the top of the picture is Apollo, ascending above a circular temple surrounded by rays of golden light. In his left hand is a statuette and he is accompanied by two genii bearing his attributes of lyre and torch. With the figure of Apollo, the whole picture seems to be caught up in an endless upward sweep of movement, to lose itself in light and infinity. On the banks of cloud on Apollo's right, the hours harness the steeds of the sun. On his left are allegorical representations of the four seasons, first Winter, shivering and wrapped in his cloak, next, with her back towards him, Ceres (summer), then Proserpina (spring) and finally Bacchus (autumn), followed by Mars and Venus, both reclining at the foot of the sun god on a grey cloud heavy with rain, which extends to the terrestial regions of the American con-

*... and Winter, by Peter Wagner, 1771–1776*

55

tinent on the shorter, northern side. The signs of the months are depicted on the zodiac circle.

A stucco figure of a giant in the left-hand corner forms the point of transition from real to imaginary space and is the prelude to the allegory of »America« above the entablature of the shorter, northern side. Indians with torches and a parrot can be seen, and in the foreground on the entablature two Titanic figures wearing turbans and a stag just killed by a hunter. Below a dark cloud, America, crowned with feathers, is riding a giant alligator, and being served chocolate by a page. The right half of the painting shows a cannibalistic camp scene; the standard bearing a griffin is an allusion to the fame of the Prince-Bishop von Greiffenklau, which had reached as far as America. Beneath this are two Indians, one of whom is carrying a silver-bellied alligator on his shoulder, while others are roasting meat on a spit over an open fire. In the background are girls bearing vessels on their heads. In the foreground above the entablature are decapitated bleeding human heads and the figure of a European observing the camp scene.

The other half of this vast fresco with its two centres comes into view as visitor starts to climb the counter-flight. »The glorification of the patron, Carl Philipp von Greiffenklau« and below, above the entablature, »Europe«, around whom the artists of the Würzburg Residence are gathered as an allegory of the arts. A medallion portrait of the patron is the focal point of this half of the painting. This rather unusual depiction of a timeless, abstract allegory where the glorification of the patron is represented by his portrait medallion transported to the heavens was borrowed by Tiepolo from an earlier German tradition. The portrait is borne aloft by Fame, complete with tuba and a geni, while a griffin, the patron's heraldic animal, clings to the lower edge of the picture frame. Saturn, with scythe and hourglass, occupies the left-hand end of the cloud-bank, while on the right is the moon goddess Diana. The medallion forms the apex of a triangle which is in a strict compositional relationship both to the allegory of the European continent below, and, through the elongated diagonal, to Mercury, messenger of the gods, who is a compositional counterpoint heralding the rise of the sun god Apollo in the other half of the picture.

The allegory of the European continent unfolds against two architectural backdrops which form the basis of this compositional triangle. The golden-haired figure of Europe is enthroned between them, listening to her musicians. All that is visible of the obligatory bull is a head garlanded with roses. The globe beside the throne is a reference to »Europe as queen of the whole world«. Pages bearing a crozier, episcopal cross and mitre allude to the bishopric of Würzburg as the centre of the arts and sciences. The arts are represented by the artists who had worked on the Residence, and in this Tiepolo departed from the character of an allegory: the fresco is a documentation, the figures representing not ideals but real people. Not all the figures can, it is true, be reliably identified. The page in a blue doublet behind the allegory of painting is probably Lorenzo, Tiepolo's younger son, while Tiepolo's own portrait is located in the left-hand corner. Pale and gaunt, with an exhausted expression, the master leans over the corner cartouche, critically examining his work. The cavalier with the powdered wig beside him is his elder son Domenico, and on the other side, as it were in contrast, is the casual, insouciant Viennese painter and gilder Franz Ignaz Roth. In the right-hand section of the painting is a man in a flowing yellow cloak standing beneath a broken pediment who from the attributes at his feet – busts, reliefs and hammer – is obviously a sculptor. This fact and his tortured expression indicate that this was probably the gifted stuccoer Antonio Bossi, who died insane in 1766. On the entab-

*Next double page:*
*The continent of Europe, from the ceiling fresco above the staircase by G. B. Tiepolo, 1753*

lature, resting like someone who has accomplished a strenuous task, sits the architect of the Residence, Balthasar Neumann, in the uniform of a colonel of the Franconian artillery. His gaze is remote and visionary, and he seems to be lost in contemplation of the vaulting of this vast hall, the stability of which was wrongly doubted by his rival Lucas von Hildebrandt. The lieutenant who is leading the big bay horse in the left-hand corner may possibly be the great architect's twenty-year-old son, Ignaz Michael Neumann.

*The continent of Asia (section) from the ceiling fresco above the staircase by G. B. Tiepolo, 1753*

Of the two remaining allegories, »Africa« is depicted on the eastern (inner) long side of the staircase, and »Asia« is on the western (cour d'honneur) side. The allegory »Africa« has two focal points. First, contrasting in composition and colour with the seated stucco giant in the left corner, the figure of a Negro with his back turned, also seated, then a group of Arab merchants and bearers with bales of goods, casks, etc. »Africa«, in the right-hand section of the painting, is a Negro princess enthroned on a dromedary. A kneeling Moor with a sun-shade swings a censer, and in the foreground are vases and elephant tusks. Negresses, a camel laden with carpets and a tent link these two groups. On the entablature in the foreground of the painting, near its centre which is marked by a medallion of an imperator, is an animal scene of a monkey plucking feathers from the tail of an ostrich. In the right-hand corner, again as a contrast to the stucco giant, is the river god Nile. The composition is linked with the allegories on the adjoining short sides by a heron in flight on the left-hand side and by the Negro princess on the right-hand side, who is pointing to the glory of the Prince-Bishop and patron.

The allegory of »Asia« on the longer side opposite is oriented towards the centre of the fresco by the ship's masts on the left and the pyramids on the right, both of which converge on the rays of the gloriole. »Asia«, en-

BATTA. TIEPOLO

throned on an elephant, is pointing like »Africa« to the portrait medallion of the patron. Before her are shackled slaves and subjects, either kissing the ground or swinging censers. In the left-hand corner men are capturing a tigress, while in the right-hand half of the picture is Calvary with crosses and pilgrims, then a pyramid and the Queen of Egypt. On the entablature in the foreground is a large block of stone with the Armenian alphabet and next to it a smaller one bearing the signature of the artist: BAT(TIS)TA TIEPOLO F. 1753.

## **4** WHITE HALL (WEISSER SAAL)

The decoration of this hall, completed between 1744 and 1745 under Prince-Bishop Friedrich Carl von Schönborn, can only be understood in relation to the other rooms in this sequence: vestibule, Garden Hall, staircase and Imperial Hall. Just as the main axes are turned by 90 degrees from room to room to give a new dimension each time, so the decoration of the White Hall, the axes of which are at right-angles to both the staircase and the Kaisersaal, is designed to contrast with the splendid colours of Tiepolo's fresco over the staircase on the one hand and with the Imperial Hall with its colour scheme of glittering gold and intense agate and violet on the other. The White Hall forms as it were a break between the two and is decorated with a deliberate absence of colour. The stucco decorations of Antonio Bossi stand out against a pale grey ground, the effect heightened by a few delicate touches of yellow and the darker grey shadows cast by the stucco reliefs. The result is an astonishingly rich and varied spectrum of white and grey tones. Antonio Bossi completed the stucco decoration for the immense wall-spaces of this hall as well the astonishingly high vaulted ceiling in only a few months, an almost unique achievement,

*White Hall with stucco-work by A. Bossi (1744/45)*

especially since the rocaille ornamentation used so lavishly here is usually found in the decoration of smaller, more intimate rooms and cabinets and is seldom as successful in monumental apartments. The stucco-work of this brilliant artist, who was to die insane, is remarkably lively and full of movement. His rocaille designs seem to blaze up, darting like flames across the vaulting and casting a trail of sparks.

The hall was originally intended as a salle de garde, as can be seen from the emblems of war and the figures of Mars and Bellona, as well as the arms of the sovereign bishopric incorporated into the stucco-work. The black-framed portraits of the prince-bishops are in deliberate contrast to the whiteness of the room. The classicist stove was made by Anton Oegg in 1769 from a model by

65

the court cabinet-maker Franz Benedikt Schlecht. The sculptures decorating the stove, an eagle and four putti representing the seasons, made of terracotta and covered in thin, gold-coloured metal, are the work of Materno Bossi, who was also responsible for the stucco-work of the niche.

*Paintings:* Portraits of Prince-Bishop Friedrich Carl von Schön-born (1729–1746; two portraits) and Prince-Bishop Anselm Franz von Ingelheim (1746–1749), all three German c. 1740/50, as well as a portrait of Prince-Bishop Adam Friedrich von Seinsheim (1754–1779) by Franz Lippold, 1755/56.

*Furnishings:* 2 console tables with the Schönborn coat of arms and 2 others, all carved and stained dark brown, Würzburg c. 1745 (workshop of Georg Adam Guthmann) ■ 2 vases, Japan, 18th century ■ 2 alabaster vases, Italy c. 1710 ■ 57 sconces with metal foliage (49 three-armed, 8 five-armed), finished in yellow lacquer, Würzburg c. 1770 ■ 5 crystal chandeliers, Vienna c. 1750.

## ■2■ IMPERIAL HALL (KAISERSAAL)

The Imperial Hall is the culmination of the magnificent sequence of apartments consisting of the vestibule, Garden Hall, staircase and White Hall. The iconography of the decoration is specifically German. Imperial halls are a typical feature of the palaces of electors and ecclesiastical rulers in the Catholic regions of Germany, and were also to be found in the residences of abbots of larger monasteries. Iconography of this kind began in the Counter-Reformation at the beginning of the 17th century, probably originating from the electoral residences in Munich and Aschaffenburg, but the tradition goes back even further, on the one hand to the Middle Ages (the strongholds of the Holy Roman Empire and the

*Imperial Hall, view of the southern half*

town halls of the free cities), and on the other to the Italian Renaissance (imperator and caesar halls).

These imperial halls were decorated according to an established iconographical and allegorical programme. This revolves around imperial galleries and the glorification of the idea of empire or the »good regime«. The Imperial Hall in Würzburg, unlike its counterpart in Bamberg, pays homage not to the House of Habsburg but rather to the concept of the Holy Roman Empire. Events were selected from the history of the old Hohenstaufen empire which also reflected the history of the Bishopric of Würzburg in a very positive light (cf. pp. 23).

The Imperial Hall, the shell of which was already completed in 1741, was only decorated and furnished in 1749–1753, under Prince-Bishop Carl Philipp von

Greiffenklau. The decoration of this unique room is the work of three equally gifted artists: the architect Balthasar Neumann, the fresco painter Giovanni Battista Tiepolo, and the stuccoer Antonio Bossi. Tiepolo and Bossi interpreted the architectural energies of Neumann's structure with their painting and stucco-work. The result is a synthesis of the arts, a work of unbelievable perfection and exquisitely harmonious colour. In the Imperial Hall, which takes up the whole width of the central pavilion on the side facing the garden (the Imperial Pavilion), the emphasis is on breadth, with accents at different points on the lower and upper levels. On the lower level the short main axis runs through the doors and windows into the White Hall and (over the balcony) into the garden, whereas the longer diagonal axis above opens out through the frescos on the narrow side into the illusionistic space of the pictures. On the ground floor the distance between the columns varies rhythmically: on the long sides they are far apart, while on the narrow sides they close up and block the central axis. The doors to the state apartments are out of line with the central axis. The result is a dynamic shift of the structural elements, thus giving the room thus life and movement. The whole of the upper level is in fact presented as an ideal sphere, as scenery. The illusionistic sphere of Tiepolo's frescos is continued into real space. The figures of followers (heralds, pages, landsknechts) move freely on the moulding and Balthasar Neumann's vaulting also rises lightly like a sail. Bossi's draperies above Tiepolo's frescos create, as it were, the illusion of a tent. The vaulting is perforated by mirrors set into it that send out sparks of light. The grisaille paintings on the lunettes and the cartouches which open up into the heavenly sphere also contribute to the fragmentary and latticed character of the vault. The frame between the frescos in the ceiling panel and the adjoining »open« cartouches is broken,

*The wedding of Emperor Friedrich I. Barbarossa and Beatrix of Burgundy, fresco by G. B. Tiepolo in the Imperial Hall, 1751/52*

*Next double page: Emperor Friedrich Barbarossa granting the Würzburg Bishop Herold the Duchy of Franconia at the Imperial Diet of Würzburg in 1168, fresco by G.B. Tiepolo in the Imperial Hall, 1751/1752*

GIO. BTTA. TIEPOLO 1750

while in other places it is overlapped and concealed by figures. The illusionistic spheres of the various ceiling frescos combine to form a single dizzying creation which spans the vaulting and then spills over into the real space of the Imperial Hall. The barriers between illusion and reality are thus blurred. The architecture becomes the stage on which the visionary historical events of the frescos are enacted.

On the southern (right-hand) narrow side is »The wedding ceremony of Emperor Barbarossa and Beatrix of Burgundy, conducted by the Prince-Bishop of Würzburg in 1156«. Here the greenish columns of the church contrast from the point of view of both colour and structure with Balthasar Neumann's agate-coloured three-quarter columns on the ground floor. In the painting the columns open out, revealing the choristers' gallery, whereas the columns of the hall below are close together, blocking the main axis. The Emperor and the fair-haired Beatrix of Burgundy kneel on the altar steps before the Prince-Bishop of Würzburg, whose features once again resemble those of the reigning Prince-Bishop von Greiffen-klau. The Chancellor of the Holy Roman Empire stands behind the couple, his sword drawn, surrounded by Roman standards and banners with the imperial eagle; a page bears the imperial crown, and a little further off stand the papal nuncio, five princes of the Holy Roman Empire and the Marshal of Franconia with the ducal sword. In the foreground to the right kneels a court dwarf, as a contrast to the figure of the bride, and on his left is her father, Rainald of Burgundy.

On the left (northern) narrow side is »Emperor Friedrich Barbarossa granting the Würzburg Bishop Herold the Duchy of Franconia at the Imperial Diet of Würzburg in 1168«. Instead of setting this scene as the programme required in the »Princes' Hall, where the estates of the Holy Roman Empire were gathered«, Tiepolo placed it

in a Mediterranean landscape, in, as it were, the Forum Romanum. Barbarossa, more like a dissipated Venetian roué with a blasé expression than an emperor, is seated on a marble throne with a shell rising behind his head like a gloriole. His right hand listlessly holds the sceptre on which the kneeling Prince-Bishop – who bears a strong resemblance to the patron Carl Philipp von Greiffenklau – is swearing the oath of allegiance. Just as the diagonal line of the sceptre is anticipated by the shaft of the banner in the Prince-Bishop's hand and the landsknecht's halbard, so the posture of the kneeling Prince-Bishop is as it were telescopically extended in three stages by the page in front of him and the landsknecht behind him, both of whom are also kneeling. Beside the throne stands the Chancellor of the Holy Roman Empire,

*The sun god Apollo conducts Beatrix of Burgundy to the Genius Imperii, ceiling fresco by G. B. Tiepolo in the Imperial Hall*

an old man of gigantic build with a prophetic air, bearing a drawn sword on his shoulder. Behind the page, who is looking down at the observer in the room below, is the Imperial Chamberlain bearing the charter of enfeoffment, standing beneath a triumphal arch with princes of the Holy Roman Empire and the Marshal of Franconia (signed: GIO.BTTA.TIEPOLO 1752).

The painting in the ceiling panel shows, on the left, the allegory of the »Genius Imperii« in the shape of the young Barbarossa, who is seated in imperial robes on a throne raised like an altar. Fame circles above him, and he is surrounded by dignitaries and the eagle banners of the Holy Roman Empire; a putto is flying towards him bearing the sword of state. The sun god Apollo approaches from the right, rising from a haze of gold and azure, bringing the bride of the Genius Imperii, Beatrix of Burgundy, in his sun chariot. Flying ahead of him is Hymen, the god of marriage, bearing a lighted torch. On the right Venus, the Franconian Ceres and the Franconian Bacchus recline on a bank of clouds.

*Page with sunshade, fresco by G.B. Tiepolo above the moulding in the Imperial Hall*

The allegories and virtues in the lunettes, painted green in green against a coffered gold background, are also the work of Giovanni Battista Tiepolo. The oil paintings above the doors, however, are by his son Domenico. Following the iconographic scheme of the Imperial Hall, these paintings depict scenes from the lives

*Emperor Justinian as lawgiver, sopraporta by Domenico Tiepolo in the Imperial Hall*

of the Roman, early Christian and Byzantine emperors: »Emperor Constantine as the conqueror of Licinius and protector of the church«, »Emperor Justinian as lawgiver«, »St Ambrose preventing Emperor Theodosius from entering a church«. In the niches on the narrow side of the hall are four extremely graceful stucco figures by Antonio Bossi: Neptune, Juno, Flora and Apollo. Above the fireplace are portraits of the patrons by Franz Lippold: Prince-Bishop Friedrich Carl von Schönborn in front of the northern tract of the Würzburg Residence (south side) and Carl Philipp von Greiffenklau (north side). Four large Viennese crystal chandeliers.

# Southern Imperial Apartments

Secretary by
K. M. Mattern,
1742
(Room 6)

**ROOMS 6 - 10**

Imperial rooms like the Imperial Hall are a typical feature of German baroque palaces. Most of the residences of the electors and ecclesiastical rulers, as well as many of the larger monasteries, had, in addition to the ruler's own rooms, sumptuously furnished state apartments which were kept in constant readiness for an occasional visit by the emperor. The decoration of these apartments alluded to their function (imperial portraits, representations of the good regime of the emperor and of the virtues etc.) The Imperial Apartments in the Würzburg Residence were especially important, as emperors regularly stayed in this bishop's city on their journey to and from Frankfurt for the coronation ceremony.

The Imperial Apartments north and south of the Imperial Hall form a single magnificent suite 160 metres in length. This enfilade (the doors arranged successively on the same axis to give an uninterrupted view from end to end) was, however, only introduced after Balthasar Neumann's visit to Paris. This is probably the reason why the doors leading to the Imperial Apartments from the Imperial Hall are placed not in the central axis of the narrow side of the hall but at the side of it. The Southern Imperial Apartments were decorated and furnished during the years 1740–1744 under Prince-Bishop Friedrich Carl von Schönborn, mainly according to his own specifications. A group of Viennese decorative artists played an important part in the decoration of the apartments: Rudolph Byss, the court painter, and his pupils Johann Thalhofer and Anton Joseph Högler, further the court potter

and porcelain maker Dominikus Eder, the court lock-smith and gifted ornamental metal-worker from the Tyrol, Joh. G. Oegg, and the Würzburg sculptor Johann Wolfgang van der Auvera, who had been trained in Vienna, the wood-carver Ferdinand Hund and, last but by no means least, Georg Adam Guthmann and his three brothers, who had probably been summoned from Munich. But these artists and craftsmen working under the aged court painter Rudolph Byss, most of whom had been trained in Vienna, were not alone in determining the style of the decorations. In this particular period their style been superseded in more than one respect by recent developments in decorative art, for in Austria, by contrast with Würzburg, the transition from baroque to rococo took place much later, if at all. Würzburg, on the contrary, this transition took place very rapidly. The great stuccoer Antonio Bossi and the sculptor, carver and designer Johann Wolfgang van der Auvera were primarily responsible for the changeover to rococo, while the influence of Bavarian rococo may also have stimulated this development.

The Imperial Apartments were destroyed by fire in 1945. Most of the stucco ceilings and frescos, as well as sections of the wall decorations which could not be removed succumbed to the flames, and some of the finest examples of rococo interior decoration in Germany were lost. All the movable furnishings and effects and some of the fixed decorations were however preserved intact.

### 6 ANTECHAMBER
### OF THE SOUTHERN IMPERIAL APARTMENTS

This room originally served as an antechamber, which accounts for the comparative simplicity of the panelling (oak with gilded beading) and the absence of ornate carving. It was also conceived in deliberate contrast to the splendour of the Imperial Hall. The wall-panelling and the gilded frames of the pier mirrors, carved by Georg Adam Guthmann in 1736 in early rococo style for a room in the original Episcopal Apartments, have been renewed, also. the stucco ceilings by Antonio Bossi, in white on a grey ground. The ceiling painting by Anton Clemens Lünenschloß (1738), »Departure of the military to capture a castle«, which was destroyed by the fire of 1945, has been replaced by the oil painting »Thank-offering«, created by Antonio Bellucci* in around 1715 for Bensberg Palace, the residence of Elector Johann Wilhelm von der Pfalz. The sopraportas with their carved gilt frames are part of the original decoration. They are the work of Giovanni Antonio Pellegrini: »Hannibal swearing eternal enmity against Rome« and »The sacrifice of Polyxena«. The original magnificent porcelain stove, the work of the Würzburg court potter and porcelain maker Dominikus Eder of Vienna, which had been transferred to this room from the First Episcopal Apartment, has been replaced by a smaller stove of the same provenance (Austria, c. 1740, possibly from Eder's circle). The lower section of Antonio Bossi's stucco-work in the stove niches has been restored.

*Tapestries:* 3 Brussels tapestries from the Alexander Cycle from cartoons by Charles Le Brun made by the manufactory of Jan Frans van den Hecke, after 1700: »Alexander the Great crossing the Granicus« (rear wall), joined in around 1745 by a woven connecting piece from the Pirot manufactory to »Battle at Arbela – Darius flees from Alexander« (entrance wall); also »Battle at Arbela – pursuit of the fleeing Persians« (exit wall).

*Furnishings:* Secretary (»Trisur«) with rich marquetry (walnut, ebony, rosewood, mother-of-pearl, ivory, brass). Master-

---

*The ceiling paintings by Antonio Bellucci here and in the following rooms are on loan from the Bavarian State Collection of Paintings, Munich.

piece by the Würzburg cabinet-maker Karl Maximilian Mattern, who worked on this splendid but heavily-proportioned piece of furniture in 1742. The gilded carvings as well as the designs for the brass engravings are by Johann Wolfgang van der Auvera. On the door, the coat of arms of the Prince-Bishop Friedrich Carl von Schönborn with the imperial crown, which, with his additional title of Prince-Bishop of Bamberg, he was entitled to include. ■ Magnificent long case clock with rich marquetry (walnut, mahogany, rosewood) and the private coat of arms of Friedrich Carl von Schönborn by Karl Maximilian Mattern, Würzburg, 1741. The gilded rococo carvings on the base and top are by Georg Adam Guthmann, the remarkable clockwork by horologer Urban Schmidt, Würzburg (clock face signed: »VRBANNS SCHMIT IN WURTZBURG Fecit«) ■ 2 console tables, carved, brown with gold, by Georg Adam Guthmann, 1742 ■ 6 banquettes (4+2), carved, brown with gold, by Johann Wolfgang van der Auvera, Würzburg, after 1750. The remarkable Gobelin coverings (flowers, fruit and rocaille work on a dark blue background) are from French models, Würzburg, Pirot manufactory, after 1750 ■ 4 and 2 sconces, two-armed, gilded bronze, by the court locksmith Johann Georg Oegg, Würzburg, c. 1745 ■ 2 crystal glass chandeliers; one of them Würzburg by Johann Michael Faller, 1760 (restored); the matching piece is new.

## ■7■ AUDIENCE ROOM
### OF THE SOUTHERN IMPERIAL APARTMENTS

This is the best preserved interior of the Southern Imperial Apartments. Only the stucco decorations by Antonio Bossi and the ceiling frescos have been renewed. The original ceiling painting by the Bamberg court painter Johann Joseph Scheubel the Elder (»Destruction of a robber baron's castle by Rudolph von Habsburg«), an allusion to the function of this suite of rooms as the Imperial Apartments, has been replaced by an oil painting by Antonio Bellucci, »The three ages of the ruler«, c. 1715. The walnut wall-panelling is original, and is inset with finely veined curlwood. The gilt rococo carvings by Ferdinand Hund, in particular the frames of the fireplace and pier mirrors, are masterpieces of their kind, with the scintillating rocaille ornamentation seeming to curl out into the room. The fireplace of violet and agate coloured marble in the French Regency style is part of the original decoration (the arms of the patron are displayed on the cast-iron chimney-plate). The sopraporta paintings, still in their original carved rococo frames, depict »Venus, Amor and Charis«, Venetian, c. 1600, and »The building of Noah's Ark« by Giacomo Bassano. The stucco marble of the stove niches has been partially renewed, while the stucco is entirely new. The large stove in Regency style by the Würzburg court potter and porcelain maker Dominikus Eder of Vienna has been replaced by a smaller rococo stove in white and gold, South German c. 1755.

*Tapestries:* 4 Brussels tapestries, three of them from the Alexander Cycle, from cartoons by Charles Le Brun: »Triumphal procession of Alexander the Great in Babylon« and »Alexander's magnanimity toward the family of Darius« (rear wall) from the manufactory of Jan Frans van den Hecke, after 1700; »Alexander's victory over King Poros of India (Part a): prisoners' procession« with the coat of arms of Prince-Bishop Johann Philipp von Greiffenklau (1699–1719), from the manufactory of Geraert Peemans, c. 1700 (entrance wall, cf. Rooms 14 and 15). Likewise from the manufactory of G. Peemans, but as early as around 1660: »Wedding of Zenobia« (exit wall).

*Doors of the Venetian Room with gilded tin decorations and paintings, c. 1740 (Room 8)*

*Furnishings:* Secretary with rich marquetry (walnut, ebony, rosewood) and the initials FC of the builder Prince-Bishop of Würzburg Friedrich Carl von Schönborn (1729–1746); Würzburg, c. 1740, possibly by Franz Benedikt Schlecht, the gilded carvings by G. A. Guthmann, the gilded bronze fittings by Johann Georg Oegg (on loan from the Bayerische Landesbank) ∎ Fireplace screen with magnificent gilded rococo carving, Würzburg, possibly by Johann Wolfgang van der Auvera, 1742/44 ∎ 4 console tables, 2 on the window piers, carved, brown with gold, by Georg Adam Guthmann, 1742, the other two carved, gilded, by Johann Wolfgang van der Auvera, Würzburg, c. 1744 ∎ 4 armchairs (3+1 copy), carved, gilded, Würzburg, 1741 by Johann Wolfgang van der Auvera. Old coverings with coarse and petit point embroidery ∎ Crystal chandelier from the same period as the orginal furnishings, French, c. 1740 ∎ 4 two-armed and 2 three-armed sconces, gilded bronze, Würzburg (probably by the court locksmith Joh. G. Oegg), c. 1740/45.

## ▣ BEDROOM OF THE SOUTHERN IMPERIAL APARTMENT (VENETIAN ROOM)

This room was originally furnished in 1738–1741 from designs by the old court painter Rudolph Byss, who, with his pupils Thalhofer and Högler, was also respon-

sible for the ceiling decoration. Here, by contrast with the other rooms, this consists not of stucco-work, but paintings in brilliant colours on a ground of polished plaster. The themes are night and sleep, in keeping with the function of the room, which in the 18th century was the imperial bedroom. (The paintings were destroyed in 1945 but have since been renewed). The wall panelling with its inset paintings, however, is original. The wood is light (»blond«) walnut with superimposed gilded tin ornamentation designed by Ferdinand Hund, which was evidently intended to give the impression of heavy, gilded bronze. The paintings inserted in the panelling have carved frames like cartouches, and are by Johann Thalhofer and Joseph Högler. In accordance with the instructions of the patron, Friedrich Carl von Schönborn, these paintings feature »symbols in the form of figures, including fruit and flowers and animals«. Fantastic beasts and comical dwarfs are found in the wainscot panelling, while figures in contemporary costume adorn the sides of the windows and the panels of the doors. There is a different iconographical programme for the sopraportas and the paintings above the pier mirrors, which feature allegories of the virtues and are the work of Georg Anton Urlaub. The blue-grey stucco marble and the gilded stucco in the stove niches have been partly renewed. The pyramid-shaped tiled stove by the Würzburg court potter and porcelain maker Dominikus Eder of Vienna, which was destroyed in 1945, has been replaced by another stove of the same stylistic provenance.

*Tapestries:* 3 tapestries from the Gobelin manufactory of Andreas Pirot in Würzburg, c. 1740–1745, with scenes from the Venetian carnival and the commedia dell'arte, from cartoons by Johann Joseph Scheubel the Elder »Carnival procession on the Piazza San Marco in Venice« (entrance wall), »Banquet in a kiosk« (rear wall), »Banquet in the open air« (exit wall).

*Furnishings:* 2 console tables, carved, brown with gold, Würzburg, c. 1740 (workshop of Georg Adam Guthmann) ■ 4 armchairs, carved, blue with gold, German c. 1741. Old coverings with gros point and petit point embroidery ■ 4 sconces, two-armed, gilded bronze, Würzburg c. 1742 by Johann Georg Oegg ■ Crystal chandelier (restored), Würzburg, by the court glassmaker Johann Michael Faller, c. 1750.

### 9 MIRROR CABINET
### OF THE SOUTHERN IMPERIAL APARTMENTS

The wall decoration of the Mirror Cabinet, completed between 1740 and 1745 and the most precious interior created in the Würzburg Residence during the reign of Prince-Bishop Friedrich Carl von Schönborn from 1729 to 1746, was completely destroyed in the bombing raids of 1945. Based on a preserved mirror fragment, numer-

View of the
Mirror Cabinet
before destruc-
tion, water-
colour by
Georg Dehn,
c. 1870

87

ous photographs and a watercolour by Georg Dehn (c. 1870/73), the entire room shell was however recreated between 1979 and 1987, resurrecting the old techniques. This reconstruction, together with the rescued furnishings, gives visitors an idea of the overwhelming effect originally produced by what was perhaps the most original work of interior decoration in the Würzburg rococo style.

Mirror cabinets are found in numerous German baroque and rococo palaces. They are usually panelled rooms with inset mirrors, carvings and stucco-work, where porcelain was frequently displayed. The walls of the Würzburg Mirror Cabinet, however, consisted entirely of glass panels, which were prepared on the back using a special technique: either paintings were made on the partially recessed mirror ground, or drawings were engraved into a gold ground that was applied on the back of the mirror, and then underlaid with dark varnish paint. By this means, instead of displaying Oriental porcelain figures in front of the mirrors as was customary, a wealth of exotic figures and scenes could be incorporated directly into the mirror. (The term »verre églomisé« used in the art trade for this and similar painting on the back of glass, originating from the name of Jean-Baptiste Glomy who died in 1786, appears inappropriate because of the much earlier origins of painting on the back of glass and because of the absence of a clear definition of the term).

For many years Prince-Bishop Friedrich Carl von Schönborn took an intense personal interest in every detail of the decoration of the Mirror Cabinet. It is possible that he decided in favour of this type of glass painting following a suggestion by Balthasar Neumann, who had earlier recommended the same technique for the panels of the wainscot in the adjacent gallery. The final concept for the Mirror Cabinet was established at an architectural

meeting in 1740 to which Friedrich Carl had invited not only Balthaser Neumann, but also the court sculptor Johann Wolfgang van der Auvera and the stuccoer Antonio Bossi.

The stuccoing of the trough vault in 1740 is one of Antonio Bossi's finest achievements. The four continents represented by allegorical female figures are the object of small scenes in the corner panels of the vault. In the centre four genii carry a huge curved mirror. These figures are in colour, sometimes with a metallically iridescent sheen. The graceful stucco ornamentation that completely covers the white background of the vault is all gilt, but with further colour accents provided by putti, heads, flowers, dragons and birds. Even the heavy gilt draperies with small mirrors set into them that billow over the moulding below seem to be influenced by the flowing movement of the entire ornamental scheme.

The versatile court sculptor and graphic artist Johann Wolfgang van der Auvera designed the concept for the figures and the ornamental decoration of the mirror walls as well as the richly carved tables with painted glass tops. The Byss disciples Johann Thalhofer and Anton Högler, together with Georg Anton Urlaub assisted by his father Georg Sebastian Urlaub and his brother Georg Christian Urlaub produced the paintings in 1741–1744 (reconstructed by Wolfgang Lenz). Except for the black marble fireplace and the white wainscot and double doors, which also have mirrors set into them (the northern doors are original), the walls consist completely of mirror and glass panels, most of them ir-

*Armchair with embroidered covering, c. 1741 (Room 9)*

90

regularly curved, whose joins are concealed by ornamental gilded stucco-work.

The observer is initally confused by the apparent dissolution of all spatial boundaries through the reproduction effect of the mutually reflecting mirror walls. The symmetry and the colour gradation of the individual glass surfaces only gradually emerge as the essential elements of the wall design. Leaving aside the unpainted mirrors, the paintings can roughly be divided into four colour combinations: gold motifs on a white ground, multi-coloured motifs on white, multicoloured on a mirror ground and gold on blue.

The four curved elongated oval mirrors in three sections to the left and right of the fireplace and on the side walls are the largest empty mirror surfaces. A few smaller pairs of similarly unpainted mirrors are located above the fireplace and on the opposite window pier, and in the remaining unequally dimensioned parts of the wall by the windows. The four large three-part wall mirrors are each »supported« by two pairs of diagonally aligned golden atlantes on a white ground; continuing outwards from these figures are four coloured ornamental panels each featuring a female bust surrounded by a floral wreath. A further ensemble of pictures grouped cruciformly around the centre mirror, painted in a variety of colours on an uncoloured mirror ground, features Chinese figures: below, noble Chinese, mostly being carried by their servants and accompanied by a retinue; above, a Chinese man and a Chinese woman on either side of an idol they are revering; to the left and right of each centre mirror and separated by it a seated noble Chinese couple. The remaining glass panels have a (probably originally even more brilliant) lapis lazuli blue background, mainly inset with gold-coloured exotic hunting scenes, jugglers, acrobats and musicians, plus occasional brightly-coloured birds or fruit. The golden plants and tendrils painted on the blue glass seem to blend with the stucco-work covering the joins between the mirrors, so that the walls appear to be covered by a fine web of golden tendrils, which simultaneously frames and binds together the individual scenes.

The walls of the two window niches depict male and female singers, dancers and musicians. The wainscot mirrors on the window side have eight scenes with animals, probably to be interpreted as symbols of vices and virtues, and on the window pier is a Chinese tea party. The coat of arms and initials of the patron, Friedrich Carl von Schönborn, appear in the middle wainscot mirrors of the side walls, flanked by two allegories of the seasons. The wainscot mirrors of the fireplace wall feature allegories of the four elements.

The plain panelled parquetry of the floor has been renewed in its old form, as has also the black marble fireplace with the Schönborn coat of arms. The inset iron chimney plates, with wrought-iron tendril ornamentation that also contains Friedrich Carl's initials, are however from the original fireplace.

*Furnishings:* Console tables, carved and gilded, with inlaid mirror pieces and glass panels painted on the back. Design and frame by Johann Wolfgang van der Auvera, Würzburg, c. 1745. ■ Games table, carved, gilded, glass top painted on the back. Design and frame by Johann Wolfgang van der Auvera, Würzburg, c. 1745 ■ Fireplace screen with elegant, gilded carving in Regency and early rococo forms, Würzburg c. 1736, by Ferdinand Hund (probably from the Second Episcopal Apartment in the south block). On the front the initials of the patron Friedrich Carl von Schönborn with the ducal coronet in gold and silk embroidery (originally with a vase with flowers in Savonnerie technique on the back) ■ 4 armchairs, carved, white with gold, German c. 1741. Old coverings with gros point and petit point embroidery on canvas ■ 2 East Asian porcelain dolls, early 18th century ■ 14 sconces (4 three-armed, 8 and 2 two-armed), gilded bronze; 10 originals by Johann Georg Oegg, Würzburg c. 1745 (restored) and 4 copies ■ Chandelier of milky-white glass with coloured glass flowers, Venice, before 1756 (restored and completed).

## 🔟 GALLERY OF THE SOUTHERN IMPERIAL APARTMENTS

In the southeastern corner of the garden front the original building already had a gallery with five window axes, which was splendidly decorated with stucco marble in 1740–1744 under Balthasar Neumann and had inset pictures surrounded by gilded stucco frames. At the beginning of the 19th century, Grand Duke Ferdinand III of Tuscany, who reigned from 1806 to 1814 as Grand Duke of Würzburg, had the gallery divided into three rooms (study, antechamber, boudoir) and completely refurnished along with the other Tuscany Rooms in Empire style (see documentation in Room 11 and 12). Since the permanent wall furnishings of the Tuscany rooms were completely destroyed by the bombing in 1945, however, the current gallery wainscotted in oak, of which only the ground plan has been reconstructed, is based on the room sequence created in the 18th century.

Three oil paintings by Antonio Bellucci, c. 1715, are inset into the ceiling, all with allegorical themes: »The pursuit of Happiness« (centre) and on either side »Allegories of the young and successful ruler«; the sopraportas, too, are not part of the original furnishings. The paintings and their carved gilt frames are Franconian and date from the mid-18th century. They depict scenes from ancient Roman history (Virtutes Romanae): »The victory of the Horatii over the Curatii« (entrance wall), »Horatius pleads for his son, who has been sentenced to death« (rear wall on the left), »Gaius Mucius Scaevola

burning his own right hand« (middle) and »The death of
Lucretia« (right).

*Tapestries:* 3 Brussels tapestries from the manufactory of
Frans van der Hecke, c. 1680, representing the months: »March
and April« (entrance wall), »July and August« and »September and October« (rear wall).

*Paintings:* Portraits of the eight prince-bishops of Würzburg
since the construction of the Residence (on the window piers
from left to right and top to bottom): Johann Philipp Franz von
Schönborn (1719–1724), first patron of the Residence; Christoph Franz von Hutten (1724–1729); Friedrich Carl von
Schönborn (1729–1746), second patron of the Residence;
Anselm Franz von Ingelheim (l746–1749); Carl Philipp von
Greiffenklau (1749–1754), who brought in Tiepolo; Adam
Friedrich von Seinsheim (1755–1779), who completed the interior and the Court Garden; Franz Ludwig von Erthal (1779–
1795), and finally Georg Carl von Fechenbach, who was the
last prince-bishop (from 1795–1802, then bishop until 1808).

*Furnishings:* 5 console tables, carved, brown with gold, the more
elaborate of these are by Georg Adam Guthmann, while the simp-
ler ones are from his workshop c. 1735–1740 ■ 8 armchairs by
Georges Jacob, Paris 1781/82 (originally from Karlsberg
Palace), carved, gilt (covering renewed), ■ Secretary by Abraham Roentgen, c. 1770. Oak veneered with maple and inlaid
with (partially coloured) boxtree, birch, amaranth and padouk ■
Three crystal chandeliers, renewed ■ Mirror, carved, gilt, Franconian, c. 1760 (probably by Johann Jakob Berg, Eichstätt).

## 11 AND 12 SERVANTS' ROOMS

An exhibition on the apartments of Grand Duke Ferdinand III of Tuscany, which were destroyed in 1945, is
currently on display in these rooms. Since the reopen-

ing of the Mirror Cabinet in 1987, the tour now returns
to the White Hall through here. The Habsburg ruler Ferdinand III (born in 1769, died in 1824), a grandson of
Maria Theresia and brother of the German Emperor
Franz II, was driven out of Tuscany by French troops and
received as compensation first of all Salzburg, and in
1805, as a result of the Peace Treaty of Pressburg, the
secularized Bishopric of Würzburg as sovereign territory. He took up occupancy of the Residence on 1 May
1806 as Grand Duke of Würzburg and reigned here for
eight years under predominantly French influence, before he was able to return to his hereditary Grand Duchy
in Florence in 1814.

Ferdinand III of Tuscany, who came to Würzburg as a
widower with young children, had three apartments fur-

nished in the Residence in the modern Empire style for himself, his future second wife and his two daughters. For economic reasons, the interior designer entrusted with the task, Nicolas-Alexandre Salins de Montfort, was instructed to take over the ground plans of three suites on the main floor more or less as they were and only redesign their appointments.

The suite of rooms (Apartment I) intended for the Grand Duke was located in the cour d'honneur and city wing of the south block. The baroque furnishings of what was known as the Second Episcopal Apartment, occupied by Friedrich Carl von Schönborn in 1737, would have looked »old fashioned« in 1805 and were probably already very worn out, so that they were not replaced. The suite of rooms intended for the future Grand Duchess in the Court Garden wing of the south block (Apartment II) began in the Southern Oval immediately adjacent to the Court Church and extended – with the three new rooms in place of the then divided gallery in the southeastern corner – as far as the Mirror Cabinet. This suite of rooms was finished first and was initially occupied by the Grand Duke himself, since Ferdinand did not remarry until after his return to Tuscany. A third modest suite of rooms (Apartment III) was furnished in the cour d'honneur wing of the north block as an apartment for Ferdinand's two young daughters.

The interior designer Nicolas-Alexandre Salins de Montfort (1753–1839), who had been educated in France, designed the furnishings of the Tuscany Rooms in Empire style. His closest associate was Ludwig Daniel Philipp Rumpf (1762–1845) from Frankfurt, a specialist in furniture manufacture and furnishing textiles. Sets of furniture were also manufactured by the cabinet-maker Johann Valentin Raab (1777–1839) and the workshop of Philipp Carl Hildebrand (1753–1805) who had died shortly before. Most of the bronze works and clocks were obtained from Paris and the glass chandeliers from Dresden.

All of the permanent wall decorations of the Tuscany Rooms were destroyed by the fire following the bombardment of Würzburg in 1945. It was only possible to restore the grotesque paintings of the Music or Dining Room in the Southern Oval (now the »Tuscany Hall« in the university area), which were completed in 1965. The remaining rooms were incorporated into the Martin von Wagner Museum and the Graphics Collection of Würzburg University, into the Gallery (Room 10), of which only the ground plan was reconstructed, and the »Charlotte Corridor« (Room 40) and its subsidiary rooms. Some of the movable furnishings – primarily seat ensembles – were however saved. The small selection of furniture and photographs displayed here documents the Tuscany Rooms and their appointments as one of the most important Empire style ensembles.

*Painting:* Grand Duke Ferdinand III of Tuscany, German, c. 1810.

## 13 CORRIDOR

The reconstruction of the Mirror Cabinet is documented in this corridor; the display includes the only preserved fragment of the original wall covering (removed in 1944 during an unsuccessful attempt at enlargement).

## 13a PASSAGE ROOM

*Paintings\*:* »Fire«, »Earth«, »Air« and »Water« by Rudolph Byss.

---

\* On loan from the Bavarian State Collection of Paintings, Munich.

# Northern Imperial Apartments

**ROOMS 14 - 21**

The Northern Imperial Apartments were decorated and furnished under Prince-Bishop Friedrich Carl von Schönborn (1729–1746), but the work was begun two years after commencement of the Southern Imperial Apartment interiors, in 1743. However, it was then hurried along so that on his election in Frankfurt in 1745 Emperor Franz I could take up residence in at least some of the rooms, albeit with provisional and somewhat simplified furnishings. The first four rooms only acquired their final character as magnificent state apartments on a par with the Southern Imperial Apartments when the decorations were substantially enriched and the stuccowork on the walls gilded under Prince-Bishop Carl Philipp von Greiffenklau (1749–1754). Nevertheless, the Northern Imperial Apartments are very different in character from their southern counterparts, for in the meantime the Würzburg artists and craftsmen had moved on from Viennese Regency decoration to Würzburg rococo. Thus the brown wood panelling, originally also planned for the Northern Imperial Apartments, was replaced throughout by stucco decoration. The range of colours used in the Northern Imperial Apartments is very much lighter, in line with the new style. The dominant colours are no longer deep browns and gold but light colours, bright red and above all white and gold. In the old inventories these rooms were, in fact, listed as »white rooms«. Against the background of these delicate and light rococo decorations, the pompous affectation of the figures in the high baroque Gobelins, which were

*Secretary by K.M. Mattern and G.A. Guthmann, c. 1745 (Room 15)*

retained from the original concept for the rooms, seems anachronistic and has an almost menacingly aggressive quality. Plans for a »Grand Cabinet« for the Empress' apartments as a counterpart to the Mirror Cabinet in the Southern Imperial Apartments, which was to have had silver decorations on a blue ground, were never carried out. The suite of »ordinari« guest rooms extending further north to the Rennweg in which, among others, Tiepolo and his sons resided from 1750 to 1753, were only furnished after the Seven Years' War under Prince-Bishop Adam Friedrich von Seinsheim (1755–1779) in the transitional style between late rococo and neoclassicism, the last room being completed only in 1771, but with little difference in style.

When the rooms were restored, only the ceiling stucco-work had to be renewed. Most of the stucco decoration in the cavetto mouldings, on the walls and framing the sopraportas and mirrors is original, likewise the sopraporta paintings.

## 14 ANTECHAMBER
### OF THE NORTHERN IMPERIAL APARTMENTS

The pure white ceiling stucco decorations by Antonio Bossi dating from 1742 have been restored. In the corners are cartouches with reliefs: allegories of the four elements (Fire, Water, Air and Earth). Three years later Bossi added the magnificent (partially restored) stucco decorations to the window and fireplace mirrors and to the sopraportas, in the flamboyant forms which characterized his late style. On the fireplace mirror: Venus and Endymion. The original ceiling painting by A. C. Lünenschloß of »The building of Würzburg Cathedral« (1741), destroyed by fire in 1945, has been replaced by an oil painting by Antonio Bellucci, »The judgement of Paris on Mount Ida with Romulus and Remus« (1715).

*Antechamber of the Northern Imperial Apartments with a tapestry by G. Peemans, c. 1700*

The paintings and surrounding decorations of the sopra-portas are original. (Entrance wall) »Genre piece«, prob-ably by Jan Cossiers; (exit wall) »Mars and Venus«, Flemish, 17th century. In place of the magnificent faience stove by the Würzburg potter and porcelain-maker Dominikus Eder of Vienna (1735), destroyed in 1945, is a Viennese rococo stove, white and gold, 1760. Blue-black marble fireplace with gilt cartouche and Schönborn coat of arms.

*Tapestries:* 3 Brussels tapestries of the Alexander Cycle with the coat of arms of the Prince-Bishop Johann Philipp von Greiffenklau (1699–1719) by Geraert Peemans, c. 1700: »Ale-xander's victory over King Poros of India (Part b): Prisoners' procession« (entrance wall), »Battle at Arbela – Darios flees from Alexander« (rear wall), »Alexander's victory over King Poros of India (Part d): Alexander's retinue« (exit wall, cf. Room 7 and 15).

*Furnishings:* 2 console tables, carved, gilded, Würzburg c. 1745–1750 (perhaps by Ferdinand Hund) ■ 5 banquettes (4+1), carved, white with gold, by Andreas Michael Dietrich. The remarkable Gobelin coverings (flowers and rocaille ornamentation on a white background) from the Würzburg Pirot manufactory, c. 1752 ■ Covered vase, octagonal with Fo dog, Japan 18th century ■ Huge blue-and-white vase, Delft, 17th century ■ 6 sconces, two-armed, gilded bronze, Würzburg, c. 1745, by the court locksmith Johann Georg Oegg ■ 2 copies of the two destroyed crystal chandeliers with coloured prisms by the Würzburg court glassmaker Johann Michael Faller (c. 1760).

*Magnificent clock by L. Hoys, Bamberg 1750 (Room 15)*

## 15 AUDIENCE ROOM
## OF THE NORTHERN IMPERIAL APARTMENTS

Only the white ceiling stucco decorations by Antonio Bossi (1742) have been restored. The gilded stucco-work dating from 1745 decorating the cavetto mouldings, the pier mirrors and the sopraportas and window niches is original. Emblems, white polished figures and the Schönborn coat of arms decorate the pier mirrors. Bossi's magnificent rocaille ornamentation also has mirrors set into it. The wood panelling is white with carved gilt ornamental. The dark, pompous compositions of the high baroque Gobelins are particularly effective against the background of this light and delicate interior, although almost aggressively so. The ceiling painting by A. C. Lünenschloß »The suppression of insurgent peasants by the Würzburg Prince-Bishop in 1525«, destroyed in 1945, has been replaced by an oil painting by Antonio Bellucci (1715) »Allegory of the princely patronage of the arts« (The liberation of Mercury by Art and Science). The paintings in the sopraportas are original: (entrance wall) »The child Moses trampling on Pharaoh's crown«, (exit wall) »Susanna and the Elders«, both by G. A. Pellegrini. In place of the splendid faience stove by

Audience Room
of the Northern
Imperial Apart-
ments
(Room 15)
the Würzburg court potter and porcelain maker Dominikus Eder of Vienna (1735), which was destroyed in
1945, there is a Viennese rococo stove, white and gold;
c. 1760.

*Tapestries:* 3 Brussels tapestries of the Alexander Cycle with
the coat of arms of the Würzburg Prince-Bishop Johann
Philipp von Greiffenklau (1699–1719) by Geraerd Peemans,
c. 1700: »Alexander's victory over King Poros of India (Part
c): The wounded Poros before Alexander« (entrance wall,
cf. Room 7 and 14), »Alexander's triumphal procession in
Babylon« (rear wall), »Alexander's magnanimity toward the
family of Darius« (exit wall).

*Furnishings:* 2 differing console tables, carved, white with
gold, Würzburg c. 1750, by the court sculptor Andreas Dietrich
■ Secretary, inlaid (grained walnut, ivory, rosewood, tin) and

carved. Masterpiece of the Würzburg cabinet-maker Karl Maximilian Mattern, the gilded carvings probably by Georg Adam
Guthmann, Würzburg, c. 1745 ■ Seat ensemble (1 sofa, 2 armchairs, 2 upholstered chairs), white with gold, carved, Würzburg 1752, by the court sculptor Andreas Dietrich. Remarkable
old Strassbourg Gobelin coverings with floral patterns on
a white background. ■ Taboret with old Gobelin covering,
c. 1720 ■ Long case clock, Würzburg, c. 1750/60, face signed
Langschwert Wirtzburg ■ Bracket clock with music mechanism (6 melodies and 9 chimes), by Leopold Hoys, signed:
LEOP.HOYS 1750 Bamberg« ■ 2 sconces, two-armed, gilded
bronze, Würzburg c. 1745, by Johann Georg Oegg ■ Crystal
chandeliers, Vienna c. 1750.

## 16 RED CABINET OF THE
## NORTHERN IMPERIAL APARTMENTS

This room in the Empress' apartments was originally intended to be a »Grand Cabinet« with silver decorations
on a blue ground (as a counterpart to the Mirror Cabinet in the Southern Imperial Apartments). The highly
imaginative and delicate stucco-work by Antonio Bossi
(partially restored) dates from this first planning phase.
In addition to the emblems of music, war, literature and
the arts, new naturalistic motifs were introduced such as
conifers, fairy-tale birds and busts. The gilded stucco
frames of the pier mirrors and sopraportas are rather
elaborate by comparison with the simple gilded carvings
of the white doors and panelling are remarkably simple.
The sopraporta paintings are original: (entrance wall)
»Moses in the bulrushes« by Sebastiano Mazzoni,
Venice, c. 1650–1660; (exit wall) »Man with jewels«;
Italian (Caravaggio school). Fireplace of agate-coloured
marble with the Schönborn coat of arms, the cast iron
stove plate dating from 1680 is from the Marienberg
fortress in Würzburg.

*Paintings\*:* 2 small landscapes by Georg Friedrich Meyer (1735–1779) ■ Landscape by Johann Franz Ermels (1641–1693) ■ Floral and fruit still life by Andreas Mattenheimer (1752–1810) ■ 2 still lifes with dead birds by Johann Albert Angermeyer (1674–1740).

*Furnishings:* 2 elegant, dainty console tables, carved, white with gold, Würzburg c. 1745/50 (probably by Johann Wolfgang van der Auvera) ■ 4 armchairs, carved, white with gold, coverings renewed, Würzburg c. 1750 ■ 2 brightly painted sconces shaped like branches with foliage and flowers, wrought-iron, Würzburg 1751, by the court locksmith Johann Georg Oegg ■ Crystal chandelier, partially renewed, Vienna, c. 1750.

## 17 GREEN ROOM OF THE NORTHERN IMPERIAL APARTMENTS

This room, which was known in the 18th century as the »Green Damask Room«, has more white in it, with relatively little gilding. While the stucco decorations on the ceiling have a light grey background, the background of the wall and mirror decorations is light green. The decorations are among the principal works of Antonio Bossi and reflect the wildly extravagant style of his later years. The rocaille work, a riot of white and gold, sparkles with light reflected from the inserted mirror fragments. Bossi's stucco-work has been preserved in its entirety in the fireplace mirror and in the sopraportas, and in part on the pier glasses, whereas the ceiling decoration has been restored. In the centre of the ceiling is »Franconia« surrounded by putti, busts and fabulous animals. On the frame of the fireplace mirror, produced a few years later, are white polished figures representing the four continents; the pier glasses are decorated with

\* On loan from the Bavarian State Collection of Paintings, Munich

106

allegories of the Occident and Orient. The original plans for a »Grand Cabinet« are reflected in the panelling and window jambs, which are not stuccoed, by contrast with the adjoining rooms, but panelled and carved, although kept noticeably simple. While it is questionable whether the sopraporta »Flora« and »Bacchus«, with frames carved by Andreas Dietrich c. 1745, can be attributed to Carlo Signani (Cignani), they are certainly the work of an Italian artist of the 17th or early 18th century. Agate-coloured marble fireplace with the Schönborn coat of arms. Wall hangings renewed.

*Paintings:* Portraits of Emperor Karl Vl (reigned 1711–1740) and Empress Elisabeth Christine by Johann Gottfried Auerbach (after Meytens), c. 1735. The frames were carved by Georg Adam Guthmann, 1736.

*Furnishings:* 2 console tables, carved, white and gold on green ground, Würzburg c. 1745 (probably by J. W. van der Auvera) ■ Pier table, carved, white and gold on a green background, Würzburg c. 1745, by Andreas Michael Dietrich ■ 4 chairs, carved, white and gold on a green background, Würzburg 1751, probably by Andreas Michael Dietrich from a design by Byss (signed: M. R. Byss); old Straßbourg Gobelin covers ■ Two andirons with horses in levade and the Schönborn coat of arms, gilt bronze, Paris, c. 1720 ■ Two East-Asian vases; Japan (Imari), 18th century ■ 4 sconces in the form of branches with foliage, two-armed, wrought-iron, Würzburg c. 1750 ■ Crystal chandelier, partially renewed, Vienna c. 1750.

*Wall clock with Chronos, originally with balancing mechanism; by M. Maerkel, Bamberg 1764 (Room 18)*

## 18 BEDROOM OF THE NORTHERN IMPERIAL APARTMENTS (NAPOLEON ROOM)

The Emperor Napoleon, who stayed in Würzburg three times during the reign of Grand Duke Ferdinand III of Tuscany, in 1806, 1812 and 1813, spent the night in this room. The state beds and bedside tables from the Tuscany Rooms were installed here for his stay in 1812 when he was accompanied by his second wife Marie-Louise, a niece of Ferdinand. The room had, however, previously been used as the imperial bedroom. The work of decoration and furnishing was interrupted by the Seven Years' War and was recommenced only in 1763. In the meantime there had been a change from Würzburg rococo to early and then late neoclassicism, which, surprisingly continued long into the seventies. During the first stage of the decoration, Antonio Bossi created the stucco-work around the edge of the ceiling (up to the dancing putti with a flower garland); during the second stage (beginning in 1763), Friedrich Manger completed the gilt central section, which has a pink-toned background. Wall hangings and bed canopy renewed. Faience stove with floral painting in burnt-in colours (partially restored); Strassbourg, by Fr. P.

109

*Bedroom of the Northern Imperial Apartments, known as the Napoleon Room
(Room 18)*

Acker, 1764. Sopraportas: »Jupiter and Mercury« (signed in the bottom right-hand corner: »Sanguinetti«) and »Mercury and Argus« by Lazaro Maria Sanguinetti; »Warrior and procuress« (rear wall) by Dirk van Baburen.

*Painting:* The portrait of Pope Benedict XIV (1740–1758) by Ignaz Stern the Younger has hung in this room since 1778.

*Furnishings:* 2 state beds and 2 bedside tables, carved, gilded, by Johann Valentin Raab, 1809 ■ 2 console-tables, carved, gilded, Würzburg by Daniel Köhler, 1771/72 ■ Seat ensemble, consisting of 1 corner sofa, 2 armchairs and 6 upholstered chairs, carved, gilded (covering replaced), Würzburg 1771/72 by Daniel Köhler ■ Wall clock with Chronos; Bamberg, by Martin Maerkel, c. 1760 (originally with balancing mechanism) ■ Ivory crucifix, South German, 17th century ■ 2 sconces, two-armed, gilded bronze, Würzburg mid-18th century ■ Chandelier with crystal prisms; Vienna, c. 1750.

Together with the bedroom, this and the two following rooms form a self-contained apartment designed for the use of highranking visitors. The wall decoration (all stucco-work) is in white and gold and also has red and green tones. Antonio Bossi worked on the first version of the decoration, while his relations Materno and Ludovico Bossi worked on the second (after 1764), which saw the transition to late rococo and early neoclassicism. In the stucco-work above the window niches are the initials AF (Prince-Bishop Adam Friedrich von Seinsheim). Naturalistic blossoms and foliate ornamentation predominate and the rocaille ornamentation is much reduced. The frames no longer describe lively, asymmetrical curves, but have become either more rigid or fully rectangular. The reliefs above the mirrors and in the corner niches depict the labours of Hercules; on the sopraportas (from left to right): »Mars and Minerva«, possibly a copy from G. de Lairesse; »Night-piece« by G. Bassano; »Cupid and putti carrying off Armour«, probably by Th. Willeborts; »The Pastrycook«, probably by A. Amorosi. Strassbourg faience stove with paintings in purple

*Secretary by A. Roentgen, c. 1768 (Room 19)*

(Hercules scenes) by Fr. P. Acker, 1766 (stove and stucco-work partially renewed).

*Tapestries:* 2 Brussels tapestries from the manufactory of Jan Frans van den Hecke; Brussels, c. 1680 with representations of the four elements: »Air and Water«, »Fire and Earth«.

*Previous double page: First Guest Room of the Northern Imperial Apartments (Room 19)*

*Furnishings:* Writing-cabinet with rocaille work, flowers, fruits and birds in coloured marquetry (mahogany, rosewood, maple, etc.), masterpiece by Abraham Roentgen; Neuwied, c. 1768 (recorded as being in Würzburg since 1778) ■ Console table, carved, gilded, Franconian, c. 1750 (recent acquisition) ■ Console table, carved, white and gold, Würzburg, 1764 by the sculptor Johann Köhler ■ Outstanding seat ensemble (1 sofa, 6 upholstered chairs) in late rococo style with wicker legs, gilded, carved, Würzburg, 1764, by Johann Köhler. Old Savonnerie covers, 1770 from the manufactory of Peter Jesse in Hei-

*Sofa by J. Köhler, 1763 (Room 19)*

delberg ■ Crystal chandelier, Vienna, c. 1740/50 ■ 4 sconces, two-armed, gilded bronze, Würzburg, mid-18th century.

**20 SECOND GUEST ROOM OF THE NORTHERN IMPERIAL APARTMENTS**

Late example of Würzburg rococo. The decorations to some extent revert to Regency art, while rocaille ornamentation is far less in evidence. The decorative frames are more solid, with no movement in them. The stucco decoration of the ceiling and walls, exclusively in white and gold, is entirely the work of Materno and Ludovico Bossi and dates from 1766/67. Above the mirrors are pairs of putti holding round paintings by the Bamberg court painter Nicolaus Treu: »Comedian with mask (entrance wall), »Old man with hourglass and book« (rear wall), »Money-counter« (exit wall) and »St Joseph with the Infant Jesus« (copy, window wall). Above the doors and false doors, rectangularly framed sopraportas (heavily restored after war damage): »Lady with violin (?)«, French, 17th century, and »Lady with faun playing a flute«, Italian, 17th century (entrance wall); »Lady with lute«, possibly by Pietro de Liberi, and »Lady at the spinet« (copy, exit wall). Fireplace of agate-coloured marble. Stucco decoration partially renewed.

*Furnishings:* The original console tables by J. P. Wagner, which were destroyed in the war, have been replaced by a table by Ferdinand Tietz (new acquisition), gilded, carved with shawms, bird net and dead birds, red marble top. Made c. 1765 for Seehof, but Tietz also worked for the Würzburg Residence ■ Seat ensemble (2 sofas, 2 armchairs, 4 upholstered chairs) in late rococo forms, gilded, carved, Würzburg, c. 1760 with renewed red damask covers ■ Stove screen, carved and gilded, Würzburg c. 1760 ■ 8 sconces, two-armed, gilded bronze, Würzburg mid-18th century ■ Crystal chandelier, Vienna, 1750.

Decorated and furnished in 1769/72 in the late Würzburg rococo style. As the corner room of the immense
garden façade, the Green Lacquered Room ends the
suite of Northern and Southern Imperial Apartments,
which has a total length of over 165 metres. It is a unique
room, a perfect reflection of late Würzburg rococo and
early neoclassicism. After the highly imaginative Mirror
Cabinet in the Southern Imperial Apartments and the
planned, though never completed Grand Cabinet in the
north block, this room is the most original if not the most
important of the typical Würzburg Residence interiors.
The special character of the room is created by its luminous green, applied on a silver ground to give the
colour depth and an unusual translucent quality, which
is vividly accented by the colours in the paintings. (The
colours of this room however suffered considerably
through the fire in the Residence in 1945). The overall
effect is heightened by the gilded stucco decorations in
late rococo forms by Materno Bossi and the paintings
of landscapes, scenes with putti, clusters of blossom,
butterflies, etc. are executed in charming colours. The
paintings in the cavetto mouldings and above the mirrors are by Georg Karl Urlaub, 1770, while those on the
walls are by Christian Popp and Ernst Schwab. The remarkable inlaid floor with its perspective pattern was
originally the work of the Bamberg court ébéniste Balthasar Hermann, who created the perplexing spatial illusion through the use of dark and light exotic woods.
(The present parquet floor is a replacement). Faience
stove with vase-shaped upper section, white with rich
gilding; Strassbourg, by Fr. P. Acker, 1766. The various
articles of furniture were designed to harmonize with
the colours of the room.

*Furnishings:* 2 console tables, green with gold, carved with putti figures by Johann Peter Wagner, c. 1770 ■ 1 sofa and 2 armchairs in Louis Seize forms, green with gold, carved, 1774 by the Bamberg court ébéniste Balthasar Hermann, who also made the original parquet floor in this room ■ Games table with marquetry (walnut, mother-of-pearl, etc.). Coat of arms of the Würzburg Prince-Bishop Adam Friedrich von Seinsheim on the table top, Würzburg, by the court cabinet-maker Franz Benedikt Schlecht, 1755–1757 ■ 8 sconces, two-armed, gilded bronze, in Louis Seize forms ■ Copy of a crystal chandelier with coloured prisms, originally by the court glassmaker Johann Michael Faller, Würzburg, c. 1760.

*Next double page: Green Lacquered Room of the Northern Imperial Apartments (Room 21)*

## 22 ■ SERVANTS' ROOM

*Paintings:* Hunting still life by Joannes Fyt (1611–1661), on loan from the Federal Republic of Germany ■ Hunting and fruit still life by Frans Snyders (1579–1657), on loan from the Bavarian State Collection of Paintings Munich.

*Furnishings:* Two commodes, inlaid, German, c. 1790 ■ 6 upholstered chairs with old French Aubusson covers, late 18th century ■ Chandelier Dresden, c. 1809.

117

# State Gallery

ROOM 23 - 29

In rooms 23–29 of the Würzburg Residence the State Gallery, which was re-opened in December 1974, presents a sequence of Venetian paintings from the 17th and 18th centuries, as well as a number of other pictures that are directly related to Venetian painting of this epoch. This is intended to supplement and draw attention to the substantial group of works of this school already in Würzburg – in particular the famous paintings of Giovanni Battista Tiepolo in the Residence.

## 23 FIRST GALLERY ROOM

2210  Johann Rottenhammer
       (Munich 1524–Augsburg 1625)
       »Adoration of the shepherds«
       (copper, 34 x 26 cm; signed and dated 1603)
In 1589 the Munich artist travelled to Italy – probably with the support of the Bavarian duke Wilhelm V. After working until the mid-1590s in the international artists' circle in Rome, in 1596 Johann Rottenhammer went to live in Venice, and in 1606 finally moved to Augsburg, where he remained until his death. The artist was strongly influenced by Upper Italian/Venetian art and was a friend of Palma Giovane; this picture is an excellent illustration of the way in which Rottenhammer took over the formal characteristics of the Italians and translated the monumental composition into the small format of the cabinet picture. According to the inscription, the picture was painted in Venice in 1603.

9330 School of Francesco Bassano the Younger
(Bassano 1549–Venice 1592)
»Venetia« (fragment), (canvas, 59 x 48 cm)
The figure, which was probably originally part of a larger composition, seems to be an allegory of »Venetia«. The sceptre, crown and luxurious garments of the young woman together with the Venetian origin of the painting, which probably dates from around 1580, suggest that the young woman is an embodiment of La Serenissima.

4227 Palma il Giovane (Venice 1544–Venice 1628)
»Lamentation of Christ«
(canvas, 153.8 x 110.8cm; signed and dated 1620)
910 »Adoration of the shepherds« (canvas, 113.7 x 96 cm)
After acquiring his first experiences as an artist in Urbino and Rome, Palma il Giovane returned to Venice at the end of the 1560s, where he soon became the leading representative of the generation of artists that succeeded Tintoretto and Veronese. His work is characterized by stylistic elements influenced by the Roman mannerists and Titian, in whose studio the great-nephew of Palma il Vecchio worked for a short time.
The »Adoration of the Shepherds«, painted in 1575, is one of the main works of Palma's early years. The loosely arranged three-dimensional scene and the fresh colours are in marked contrast to the »Lamentation of Christ«; this type of devotional picture, which calls on the observer to contemplate the sufferings of Christ, first appeared in the Middle Ages. Since the heavy colours and the close arrangement of the figures indicate that this was one of the artist's late works, the inscription should probably be read as 1620.

3679 Lodewijk Toeput, called Pozzoserrato
(Antwerp c. 1550–Treviso c. 1605)
»Landscape with view of a city«
(canvas, 48 x 96 cm)

The Flemish artist Lodewijk Toeput probably went to Italy in around 1573, and worked in Venice, Florence and Rome before settling permanently in Treviso in 1582. While his most important achievements are in the area of landscape painting, Pozzoserrato's imaginary compositions with accessory figures identify him as one of the main representatives of a style of painting that combines both northern and southern influences. This painting is an example of this style, with an unusual mixture of very different Italian and Dutch motifs.

**2734**  Pietro Muttoni, called della Vecchia
(Venice 1603–Venice 1678),
»Portrait of a man« (canvas, 110 x 100 cm)
Pietro Muttoni, who was also a musician and a writer, was already famous amongst his contemporaries for his imitation of the great 16th-century painters. This portrait of a man is also faithful to the tradition of Upper Italian/Venetian portrait painting. While the sparing architectonic setting and the way the three-quarter-length portrait fills the frame show the influence of Giorgione and Titian, the animated, speaking figure captured at a particular moment is reminiscent of Lorenzo Lotto. The unusual clothing raises the question as to whether this is really a portrait or a representation of a character or role.

**24 SECOND GALLERY ROOM**

**2285**  Giovanni Battista Piazzetta (copy)
»Assumption of Mary« (canvas, 146 x 70 cm)
Giovanni Battista Piazzetta (1683–1754), working in Venice, produced a monumental altar painting of the »Assumption of Mary« for the Elector and Archbishop of Cologne, Clemens August von Wittelsbach (1700–1761), which was installed in 1736 in the church of the Teutonic Order in Frankfort on the Main and is now in the Louvre.

The popularity of Piazzetta's picture in the 18th century is testified by the numerous contemporary copies of this composition. While it is not known who produced this particular, smaller version, the rendering of the figures indicates that the work was a direct copy of the original.

**10376** Giovanni Antonio Pellegrini
(Venice 1675–Venice 1741)
»Irene rescuing St Sebastian« (canvas, 228 x 170 cm)
Giovanni Antonio Pellegrini left his home town in 1708 and went first to England and then, in 1713, to Düsseldorf where he was engaged by Elector Johann Wilhelm von der Pfalz (1658–1716). After the death of the Elector, the artist worked at various European courts before returning to Venice in 1737.
The Roman officer Sebastian, persecuted for his Christian faith and sentenced to death by Emperor Diocletian, survived the first attempt by the archers of his own company to execute him. Left for dead, the martyr was found by the Christian Irene and her companion who nursed him back to health; shortly afterwards he finally fell victim to his persecutors. As the (possibly later) inscription on the left reveals, this typical 18th-century painting was produced during Pellegrini's stay in Düsseldorf.

**H. and W. 33** Giovanni Battista Pittoni
(Venice 1687–Venice 1767)
»The sacrifice of Polyxena«
(canvas, 133 x 161 cm)
**H. and W. 32** »The magnanimity of Scipio«
(canvas, 134 x 161 cm)
Giovanni Battista Pittoni, who worked for many European courts and numerous clients in Italy, had schooled himself on the Venetian masters and in 1758 advanced to become the head of the newly-founded Venetian academy. »The magnanimity of Scipio« and »The sacrifice of

Polyxena« are two themes from the ancient world that were popular with 18th century artists.

According to the Roman historian Livius, Publius Scipio captured a girl of particular beauty during his campaigns in Spain. When, however, he heard of the young woman's engagement, he returned her to her bridegroom together with all the ransom money and asked merely for the friendship of the couple and their families in return. – Polyxena, daughter of the Trojan king Priamo, met a different fate: her hand was sought by the Greek Achilles during the Trojan War, and Achilles promised the king that if she became his wife, the Greeks would withdraw from Troy. However, after Achilles had been fatally wounded by Polyxena's brother Paris, he demanded before he died that Polyxena be sacrificed on his grave after Troy had been conquered. Achilles' son Neoptolemos fulfilled this cruel promise and had Polyxena killed.

*»Irene Rescuing St Sebastian«, painting by G. A. Pellegrini, Düsseldorf 1713 (Room 24)*

**11336** Federico Bencovich
(Dalmatia (?) c. 1677– Gorizia 1753)
»Hercules and Omphale« (canvas, 130 x 107.50 cm)
Federico Bencovich, who was strongly influenced by the art of Venice and Bologna, ranks as one of the leading representatives of Upper Italian Settecento art. From 1715 on, Bencovich, who was in the meantime living in Vienna, received orders from high-ranking German clerics. He worked for Lothar Franz von Schönborn, Prince-Bishop of Bamberg and Elector and Archbishop of Mainz, in the ruler's Weißenstein Palace near Pommersfelden. In 1734 he was appointed court artist by Friedrich Carl von Schönborn, Bishop of Bamberg and Würzburg, and produced various paintings for his Würzburg Residence and Court Chapel. The subject of this painting, taken from ancient mythology, had been popular as an example of »female power« since the Renaissance. As punishment for slaying his guest Iphitos, Hercules was sold to Omphale, the

Queen of Lydia. Because he fell in love with her, even though he was forced to act as her slave, the reversal of roles shown here – the ancient hero with spindle and distaff, Omphale wearing a lionskin and bearing a club – is not without erotic connotations.

## 25 THIRD GALLERY ROOM

914 Antonio Bellucci (Venice 1654–Venice 1726), »Danae and Perseus on the raft« (canvas, 123 x 176 cm)

915 »Amor and Psyche« (canvas, 111 x 170 cm)

Antonio Bellucci was one of the first »travelling artists« who spread the Venetian decorative style throughout Europe. The Venetian-born Bellucci spent some time in Vienna, Düsseldorf and finally also in England, where he worked on the interior of Buckingham Palace. He produced the two allegories of love in Düsseldorf for the Elector Johann Wilhelm von der Pfalz (1658–1716). After the birth of Perseus, fathered by Zeus disguised as golden rain, Danae and her son were banished by Danae's father, who doubted the god's paternity. Zeus however watched over the dangerous journey and enabled the two to reach the island of Seriphos unharmed. Bellucci depicts the young Perseus playfully guiding the raft over the foaming waves. Psyche, by contrast, is depicted with a dagger, intent on murdering her lover Amor. Psyche was forbidden to look at Amor, who visited her every night; her envious sisters convinced her he must be a monster. When Psyche approached her lover at night with the dagger, however, she saw how beautiful he was. But Amor awoke and fled.

## 26 FOURTH GALLERY ROOM

H. and W. 31 Marco Ricci (Belluno 1676–Venice 1729) »Architectural caprice« (canvas, 90 x 72 cm)

Marco Ricci, pupil of his famous uncle Sebastiano Ricci (1659–1734), worked primarily in Venice and Upper Italy as a landscape painter. Unlike Sebastiano, whose compositions were dominated by figures, Marco Ricci became famous as the inventor of imaginative architectural caprices. A number of works provide evidence that nephew and uncle also produced paintings together. This architectural caprice (capriccio) by Ricci lives up to its name as a work of creative fantasy. An imposing setting of ancient architectural ruins and relief fragments is enlivened by a few accessory figures; in the distance beyond the already overgrown ruins a Gothic building can be seen. The architectural ensemble is not based on reality but is a purely imaginary invention of the artist.

**5888** Antonio Canaletto (school)
»View of the Canal Grande from San Vio«
(canvas, 138 x 197 cm)
**5914** »St Mark's Square in Venice« (canvas, 139 x 97cm)
Both vedutas, the »View of the Canal Grande from San Vio« and »St Mark's Square in Venice« are copies of what were evidently highly esteemed works of Antonio Canaletto (1697–1768). Views of the city of Venice were very popular with travellers broadening their education in the 18th century, in particular the English; they bought them as a souvenir of their visit to La Serenissima. Canaletto succeeded not just in realistically depicting the buildings of the various districts, but also in capturing the particular atmosphere of the lagoon city. Familiar motifs were much in demand, such as St Mark's Square with the façade of the church or the Canal Grande with its palazzi and colourful gondolas.

**1451** Pietro Rotari (Verona 1707– St Petersburg 1762)
»Friedrich Christian, Electoral Prince of Saxony«
(canvas, 107 x 86 cm)

**4485** »Maria Antonia of Bavaria, wife of Friedrich
   Christian, Electoral Prince of Saxony«
   (canvas, 97 x 72 cm)

The wedding of Friedrich Christian of Saxony (1722–
1763) and Maria Antonia of Bavaria (1724–1780) took
place in Dresden in 1747. Pietro Rotari, who came to Dresden a few years later by invitation of the Saxon Elector August III, recorded the stately appearance of the Electoral
Prince and his consort in almost life-size portraits. In spite
of the baroque setting, with his sparing but delicate colours
and psychological insight Rotari succeeds in conveying the
character of his subjects. Friedrich Christian was already
a determined reformer of domestic and foreign policy even
before he became elector in the autumn of 1763. He died
shortly afterwards, however, in 1763, and never experi-
enced the rebuilding of Saxony after the Seven Years' War.
Maria Antonia is one of the most educated regents of her
time. As well as speaking five languages, she was an ama-
teur writer and also painted and composed. The matching
portraits probably date from 1754, as indicated by the
publishing year of the book lying in front of Maria Antonia.

**27 NORTHERN OVAL GALLERY HALL
   (FORMER OPERA THEATRE)**

There is nothing left in the room that has been used since
1931/32 as the Gallery Hall to indicate that the 21.5 x 15 m
rotunda built under Prince-Bishop Adam Friedrich von
Seinsheim was originally an opera theatre, the »pretty little
theatre in Würzburg«, as it was described by his brother.
It was first planned as a princes' hall, and François Cuvilliés the Elder had delivered a wooden model for the interior in 1766, but this idea was abandoned. The theatre interior, designed in the form of an amphitheatre with three
rows of seats, a prince's box and a west-facing stage oc-
cupying well over a third of the major diameter of the

room, was removed as early as 1790 under Prince-Bishop Ludwig v. Erthal due to lack of use. The name »Old Library« (1820) was finally replaced in the course of the 19th century by »Merry-Go-Round Hall«: when the Crown Prince and subsequent King Ludwig I and his court resided in Würzburg, a merry-go-round was set up here, which had been built during the reign of Grand Duke Ferdinand III of Tuscany (1806–1814) for the Werneck Summer Palace and is today located in the Marstallmuseum in Nymphenburg Palace in Munich.

Veronese studio

455 »Fides and Spes« (canvas, 207 x 132 cm)
445 »Caritas« (canvas, 207 x 133 cm)
527 »Fortitudo and Temperantia« (canvas, 207 x 133 cm)
447 »Justitia and Prudentia« (canvas, 207 x 133 cm)

The cycle from the Veronese studio consists of four pictures with allegories of the virtues: in addition to the three theological virtues Fides, Spes and Caritas, the four cardinal virtues Justitia, Prudentia, Fortitudo and Temperantia are also portrayed as female figures. While Fides (Faith) is identified with the chalice, which is a reference to the Sacrifice of the Mass, Spes (Hope) is depicted in prayer without any particular attributes; this was the usual representation of this figure in Italy, although the snakeskin on her head may be a reference to the overcoming of heresy. Caritas (charity) is personified by a motherly woman attending to three children who have their arms around her. Fortitudo (Fortitude) is paired here with Temperantia (Temperance) and Justitia (Justice) with Prudentia (Prudence), and they are clearly identified by their attributes. Fortitudo is depicted with a column, seated opposite Temperantia whose attributes are two vessels for mixing water and wine. Justitia is depicted with the scales of justice while the mirror in the hand of Prudentia represents critical self-analysis.

**2621** Joseph Heintz the Younger
(Augsburg c. 1600 – Venice 1678)
»Il Ridotto« (canvas, 136 x 163 cm)

**3657** »Contest at the Ponte dei Pugni« (canv., 135 x 192 cm)
After his training in Augsburg, Joseph Heintz the Younger went to Venice, where he is known to have lived from 1625 on. In Italy the German artist became well-known for religious themes and also for his depiction of festivities and popular entertainments. The portrayal of social events with Venetian backdrops was very popular in the 18th century and was perfected by artists such as Francesco Guardi and Antonio Canaletto. Heintz also became a chronicler of Venetian life: while »Il Ridotto« is a record of the opening of the casino in the palazzo of Marco Dandolo in 1638, the subject of »Ponte dei Pugni«, is a traditional boxing match between two hostile municipal districts. Both paintings are typical examples of Heintz's densely peopled, often bizarre depictions of Venetian life.

**1264** Claudio Ridolfi (studio)
»Queen Jezebel is thrown to the dogs«
(canvas, 213 x 323 cm)
This rarely depicted scene is a story from the Old Testament (2 Kings, 9, 30-37): because she had prophets assassinated and worshipped Baal of Tyre, Queen Jezebel was accused of idolatry and thrown from a window of her palace by order of King Jehu. As it had been prophesied, her body was eaten by dogs. The painting recently ascribed to Claudio Ridolfi (c. 1570–1644) sets the scene against an elaborate architectural backdrop. In typical 17th-century style, the scene is peopled with many additional figures. The theatrical setting conveys nothing of the horror of this event.

**12505** Leandro Bassano (Bassano 1557–Venice 1622)
»Portrait of Giovanni Magnani of Pisa«
(canvas, 87.8 x 68.4 cm)

**8091** »Portrait of the merchant Leonhard Herrmann«
(canvas, 133.4 x 95.5 cm)

Leandro was a member of the highly productive dal Ponte artist family, who were known by the name of Bassano after their place of residence from the late 16th century on. After training with his father, the famous Jacopo Bassano (1510/15–1592), in 1588 he settled permanently in Venice. Leandro painted altar pictures and religious topics, but was well-known in particular for his portraits. After the artist had painted portraits of the Venetian doge Marino Grimani and his wife, he was rewarded by the former with the title of »Cavaliere di S. Marco«. Giovanni Magnani of Pisa is identified by the name on the letter he holds in his right hand. Dark clothing, a coat loosely draped over his shoulders, a gold ring and discreetly visible gold chain as well as a pair of gloves identify the subject as a prosperous, respected member of the nobility. – The German merchant Leonhard Herrmann was in Venice between 1571 and 1582; in 1571, he held the office of consul at the Fondaco dei Tedeschi, the trade mission of the German merchants in the lagoon city. Herrmann is depicted in the fur-trimmed coat that was the representational garment of the 16th century, in the process of writing a letter. While the quill, inkpot, scissors and paper are references to his commercial activity, the hour-glass is a symbol of earthly transience. The memento mori symbol is also an indication of the function of the portrait as a memorial.

*Next double page: »Rinaldo under the Spell of Armida«, painting by G. B. Tiepolo, Würzburg 1753 (Room 13c)*

**28** FIFTH GALLERY ROOM

**478** Domenico Fetti (Rome c.1588/89–Venice 1623),
»Ecce Homo« (canvas, 80.7 x 64 cm)
**H. and W. 28** Domenico Fetti (studio)
»Jacob's dream« (canvas, 60.5 x 45 cm)

The young Domenico Fetti attracted the attention of Ferdinand II Gonzaga at the outset of his career in Rome, and

was summoned by him to Mantua in 1613/14 to be court artist; in 1622 Fetti left this town and went to Venice. This »Ecce Homo« probably originates from Gonzaga's collections. Christ, crowned with thorns and presented to the people by Pontius Pilate with the words »Ecce Homo« (Behold, the man! John 19,5), is depicted here as a single figure behind a balustrade, with an inscription that speaks directly to the observer: I have suffered this for you, but what have you done for me?) Removed from its scenic context, the picture summons the faithful to contemplate the suffering of Christ. – »Jacob's dream« is a studio reproduction of the original painted by Fetti in around 1615/16 and now in the Kunsthistorisches Museum in Vienna. It depicts the scene described in Genesis 28, 10–17, where Jacob, fleeing from his brother Esau, spends the night in an open field. In a dream he sees a ladder on which angels are ascending and descending. At the top of the ladder stands God the Father, who blesses Jacob and promises his descendants the land on which Jacob has laid down to rest.

**10645** Carlo Innocenzo Carlone (Scaria 1686–Como 1775)
»The beheading of John the Baptist«
(canvas, 47.5 x 73 cm)

After training in Venice and Rome, Carlo Innocenzo Carlone was soon primarily active north of the Alps, where he became the favourite artist at numerous courts. In 1715 he moved to Vienna, where he remained for many years. Numerous secular and sacred paintings of Carlone's have been preserved; the artist was particularly valued for his frescos, which depicted the ceremonial court life of the time. As the spontaneous brush strokes and the blank spaces in the corners indicate, this small oil sketch (Bozzetto) is a preliminary study. The same composition can be found on the ceiling of the parish church of Groß-Siegharts in Lower Austria, where it was painted by Carlone in 1727.

**1122**  Giambettino Cignaroli (Verona 1706–Verona 1770),
»Adoration of the Kings« (canvas, 47 x 70 cm)

Giambettino Cignaroli was first influenced by the Seicento artists of Verona and Bologna; he then moved to Venice where he lived from 1735 to 1738 and was stimulated by the great masters of the 16th century such as Paolo Veronese and Giambattista Tiepolo. After his return in 1739, Cignaroli was much in demand as an artist in Verona and produced a large number of sacred paintings. His reputation is testified by the commissions he received from the electors of Saxony, Katharina II and Stanislaw II of Poland, and the visit paid to him by Emperor Joseph II when he was in Verona in 1769. In accordance with the tastes of the times, Cignaroli's »Adoration« fills the whole picture with numerous figures and enlivening narrative details.

**1590**  Johann Anton Eismann
(Salzburg 1604–Venice 1698)
»Coastal scene« (canvas, 64 x 87 cm)

After working as an artist for the Bavarian electoral court in Munich and studying mathematics, Johann Anton Eismann went to Italy, where he lived first for several years in Rome and then settled permanently in Venice in 1663. Landscapes, battle scenes, seascapes and caprices were the main themes of his paintings. Eismann modelled this coastal scene on Dutch seascape painting, but added typical Italian elements such as the Venetian galley and the ruin of a large castle. This imaginative scene does not thus represent a specific coast, but combines the various picturesque elements of Mediterranean harbours.

## 30 SERVANTS' ROOM ADJOINING THE INGELHEIM ROOMS

*Painting:* »Summer landscape«, by F.H. Paradyen, 1749.

# Ingelheim Rooms

## (FIRST EPISCOPAL APARTMENT; SEINSHEIM ROOMS)

ROOMS 31 – 38

The interior decoration of the Ingelheim Rooms (1776–1781, the last major project of the 18th century, also brought to a close the building and furnishing of the Residence, which had continued without interruption for almost 60 years. As the work of the court stuccoer Materno Bossi – in cooperation with the court sculptor Joh. P. Wagner (furniture) – they form the stylistic highpoint of the Seinsheim era (1775–1779). In 1898 they were already being praised as »one of the finest works of early neoclassicism in Germany« (B. Renard). After the fire in 1945, the partially destroyed ceilings and floors were reconstructed, the damaged walls were restored and completed and in 1978 the whole apartment was reopened with the furniture that had been saved and also restored.

*Hall of the Ingelheim Rooms with the portrait of Friedrich Carl von Schönborn (Room 31)*

All that associates the eight rooms in the city wing of the north block with Prince-Bishop Anselm Franz von Ingelheim is their name; during his short reign (1746–1749), the successor of Friedrich Carl von Schönborn lived in complete seclusion in the suite of rooms with the small hall. All the other prince-bishops lived in what was known as the Second Episcopal Apartment that existed in the cour d'honneur and city wing of the south block from 1737 (later Apartment I of the Tuscany Rooms, now Martin von Wagner Museum).

Ingelheim's brief residence here in any case had no influence on the interior decoration and the furnishing of these rooms, which was begun 20 years earlier and not completed until 30 years after Ingelheim's reign. The First

Episcopal Apartment had already been commenced here under the first patron Joh. Phil. Franz von Schönborn (1719–1724) and continued by his successor Chr. Franz v. Hutten (1725–1729) – when the Court Chapel in the north block was also planned – but it had not quite been finished at the time of Hutten's death. A fireplace (Room 37) and the stuccoed ceilings and cavettos of five rooms created in Regency style by Johann Peter and Karl Anton Castelli in 1724–1725 have remained from this period. Completed immediately after Balthasar Neumann's first stay in Paris, they are the oldest preserved stucco decorations in the Würzburg Residence.

At the same time, the Ingelheim Rooms also contain the most recent original interior decoration of the palace; this was commissioned by Prince-Bishop Adam Friedrich v. Seinsheim (1755–1779) from the court stuccoer Materno Bossi in 1776 and determines the present appearance of the suite of rooms. After the halls of the north block (Opera Theater in the Northern Oval, Princes' Hall), the rooms were upgraded and now provided, in addition to the state rooms on the garden side, »yet another place for holding dinners and social gatherings«, as was stated on the occasion of their first use in 1778. Their simultaneous function as a guest apartment is revealed by the description of the room in the inventory of 1778: the new red hall, and on either side of it: antechamber, bedroom, cabinet, valet's room.

Although the Ingelheim Rooms give an overall impression of uniformity, the various elements of the early neoclassical room decorations differ considerably from one another. Their most evident feature, their colourful appearance – silvered stucco on coloured wall surfaces – were the result of Seinsheim's connections with Munich (Munich Residence, Amalienburg and Schleißheim Palace). In 1776 the stuccoer visited Munich to study the work there. The uniform use of stucco is line with the general trend already evident in the northern state rooms; the sopraportas are decorated not with paintings but with stucco reliefs of outstanding quality by Materno Bossi. As in the gardens of the Seinsheim era, the reliefs are dominated by putti.

For the individual stucco decorations, Bossi partially incorporated the stucco ceilings of the first phase of decoration and used them as his models and source of inspiration, as shown, for example, by Room 33 which takes up the theme of music again and Room 36 with its floral motives. The continental symbols in the hall (Room 31), were even influenced by G. B. Tiepolo's staircase fresco. And the entire content of the hall decoration reflects the fresco programme of the staircase.

In addition to these references to older models, French engravings in Louis Seize style were also used in accordance with the prevailing tastes; these give the Ingelheim Rooms their characteristic appearance and distinguish them from the decorations at the end of the rococo era, and from the brief phase of early goût grec in the northern state rooms. The Würzburg court stuccoer used the Nouvelle Iconologie Historique of Jean Charles Delafosse, which appeared in Paris in 1771. The decoration models contained in it are intended to express symbolic meanings and are of correspondingly unusual design (see Plate on page 141). Even though Bossi used these models without regard to their meaning, they have kept their unique Delafosse character. This is reflected by the motifs, sometimes of a grotesque nature, such as masks, flat-tailed fish, cornucopias with luxuriant fruits, etc., which are taken from the abundant forms of 16th-and-17th-century French decorative art, but also by the frequently unusual setting of these motifs, suggestive of mannerism: here decoration motifs are given architectural forms and architectural elements acquire a decorative purpose. The furniture of the Ingelheim Rooms, such as the stoves delivered from Vienna and some of the furniture made by the court sculptor Joh. P. Wagner is also influenced by Delafosse models.

The Ingelheim Rooms are thus the main example of the Delafosse style (Main-Franconian version), which replaced the goût grec in the Residence as a short-lived variation of the Zopfstil. For the last time, room decoration and appointments were conceived as a synthesis of the arts, but also linked directly with the previous epochs of decoration since the Residence was begun.

## 31 HALL OF THE INGELHEIM ROOMS

The Hall occupies the middle three window axes and – by contrast with the apartments on either side – the entire depth of the city wing of the north block. The elevated flat ceiling and the round-arched windows on both sides give it the character of a hall. The decoration on the walls and ceilings, which is all stucco-work, was created by the court stuccoer Materno Bossi from 1776 to 1778 using the engraved patterns (Plate, picture on the right) of the French architect Jean Charles Delafosse. – After the damage suffered in the war, restoration of the interior shell of this room and the adjoining apartments was completed in 1978.

The stucco decoration celebrates the person and the reign of the patron, Prince-Bishop Adam Friedrich v. Seinsheim: above the stove in the middle of the end wall is his coat of arms, and on the opposite wall his likeness as a relief medallion, each flanked by two caesarean busts as a symbol of glorious apotheosis. The real message is contained in the middle ceiling section, where a customary image was used equating the prince with the sun; as »sun of the country« he is the source of prosperity for the country and his subjects as the sun is the source of light and warmth. Under his rule, trade flour-

*Engraved model for the stucco-work of the window piers in the Hall of the Ingelheim Rooms. From the Nouvelle Iconologie Historique of J. Ch. Delafosse, Paris 1771*

141

ishes and the arts prosper. This is represented by the initials AF in the sun on the ceiling, by the four continents above the mirrors, by the depictions of science and commerce, architecture, sculptural art and painting in the reliefs above the doors as well as on the ceiling and by the musical instruments and the relief busts, which probably represent female singers and musicians.

The programme thus clearly follows that of the staircase fresco by G. B. Tiepolo, and the stuccoer used similar forms in his successful rendering of the four continents as puttos.

With the state portrait of the Prince-Bishop Friedrich Carl v. Schönborn (1729–1746) on the southern end wall, Seinsheim honours the ruler who was his model and at the same time refers to the fact that his uncle had been the first to live, briefly, in the Ingelheim Rooms – even though this was only a provisional measure – 40 years earlier.

*Painting:* State portrait of Prince-Bishop Friedrich Carl v. Schönborn (reigned from 1729 to 1746), full length, pointing to Schönborn Palace near Göllersdorf (repetition of the portrait in the Princes' Hall).

*Furnishings:* 2 x 2 console tables, Joh. P. Wagner, 1776/1780, painted white and silvered. Two tables, already bearing the initials of Prince-Bishop Franz Ludwig v. Erthal ■ 6 chairs, Joh. P Wagner, 1776/1780, painted white and silvered, red silk damask covering renewed ■ 8 taborets, in the same design ■ 4 bronze statuettes on Boulle plinths, allegories of the 4 elements, Paris c. 1725 ■ 24 sconces (8 five-armed, 16 three-armed) with metal foliage, originally from a design by Materno Bossi (replaced) ■ 8 sconces on either side of the mirrors, three-armed, probably originally from a design by M. Bossi, cast brass (replaced) ■ 2 glass chandeliers with crystal pendants.

## 32 RED ANTECHAMBER OF THE
## INGELHEIM ROOMS (HUNTING ROOM)

The silvered stucco decorations on a pale red background were completed in two phases, with a gap of around 50 years. The stucco-work of the cavetto, including the corner cartouches, was designed by the stuccoer Joh. P. Castelli to the specifications of the Parisian architect German Boffrand and produced »from the drawing of the hunt« in 1724–1725 for the First Episcopal Apartment. The stucco-work on the walls and the ceiling rosette, however, is Zopfstil ornamentation and was created in 1776–1778 during the Seinsheim era by the court stuccoer Materno Bossi. For his work he used the engraved models in Jean Charles Delafosse's Nouvelle Iconologie Historique; the motif above the mirror, for example, is taken from the model entitled »Abissinie ou haute Ethiopie et la Religion«. The hunting theme which gave the room its name was also incorporated in the second decoration phase, as shown by the sopraporta reliefs with the three hunting scenes by Bossi. They show fishing, the hunting of game birds and the hunting of hares using hawks. The faience stove from Vienna matches the style of the wall decoration.

*Furnishings:* Console table, G. A. Guthmann, c. 1740, painted pale red and silvered ■ 6 upholstered chairs, Joh. P. Wagner, 1778/1780, painted pale red and silvered, silk damask covering matching the colouring of the wall coverings (renewed) ■ Commode with two drawers, Franconian, c. 1785. Veneered with walnut and walnut root ■ Secretary belonging to Prince-Bishop Franz Ludwig v. Erthal, Main-Franconian, c. 1780. Veneered and inlaid with walnut, walnut root, mahogany, rosewood and palisander, gilded bronze fittings. The front of the upper section can be folded down for use as a writing surface and the middle pilaster with the initials FL functions as the support. Inside, the upper section can be closed with a partition that operates like a roller blind. Lower section with doors at the side and drawers behind them. The counterpart of this secretary belonging to the Mainz Elector Friedrich Carl v. Erthal is located in Aschaffenburg Palace ■ Ivory sculpture »The sacrifice of Isaac« by Simon Troger, Munich, c. 1760 ■ Bronze statuette of Diana by court sculptor Claude Curé, Würzburg, 1724. Plinth signed: »Claud Curé scul: J:A: Roth fud: 1724« ■ 2 sconces, three-armed, originally probably designed by M. Bossi, cast bronze (renewed) ■ Glass chandelier with crystal pendants.

## 33 GREEN WRITING ROOM OF THE INGELHEIM ROOMS (MUSIC ROOM)

In this room too, the stucco-work commenced under Prince-Bishop Johann Philipp Franz v. Schönborn in the first decoration phase of the Residence is combined with that of the Seinsheim era: Joh. P. Castelli produced the stucco-work of the ceiling and cavetto in Regency style in 1724–1725, designed to the specifications of Germain Boffrand. Music is the theme of this decoration, with representations of various instruments, and this also gave the room its name. Over 50 years later, in 1776 to 1778, Materno Bossi created the Zopfstil decoration of the walls with the dominant motif of the bucranium (steer skull) with the laurel wreath above a rosette frieze; his model was »Siam et la Religion« from the Nouvelle Iconologie Historique of Jean Charles Delafosse. The theme of the Regency decoration was taken up again by Bossi, not in the sopraporta reliefs, which depict bowls of fruit, but in the window niches with the hanging arrangements of musical instruments. The faience stove from Vienna matches the style of the wall decoration.

*Tapestries:* 3 tapestries with depictions of country life based on motifs by David Teniers. Entrance wall: Skaters and hog slaughtering, Brussels, Le Clerc, c. 1710. Rear wall: The fish catch, Brussels, signed »ACASTRO« (= van der Borght), c. 1710. Exit wall: Archery, Lille (?), c. 1680.

*Furnishings:* Seating ensemble, consisting of 2 upholstered chairs, 4 armchairs (Bergères) and a two-seat sofa, Joh. P. Wagner, 1778/1780. Painted pale green and silvered to match the room shade, coverings in greenish silk damask, renewed ■ Console table, G. A. Guthmann, c. 1740, painted green and silvered ■ 2 commodes with two drawers, Main-Franconian, c. 1780, veneered in grained birch and walnut, oval medallion with inlaid musical instruments on the front ■ 2 alabaster groups of battling gladiators by Joh. W. van der Auvera, Würzburg, l738. The group with the net combatant is signed on the plinth: »I. WOL: V. AUWERA. F: 1738« ■ 2 sconces, three-armed, originally probably from a design by M. Bossi, cast brass (renewed) ■ Glass chandelier with crystal pendants.

## 34 YELLOW CORNER CABINET OF THE INGELHEIM ROOMS

The room facing the Rennweg and the Rosenbach Palais with its silvered stucco-work against a yellow background also reflects the two different phases of decoration in Regency and Zopfstil. On the ceiling and the cavetto are the decorations created in 1724–1725 by Joh. P. Castelli for the First Episcopal Apartment, whereas the stucco-work of the walls was completed in 1776–1778 by Materno Bossi. The decorations around the fireplace and the elaborate floor pattern made of different-coloured woods (renewed) are both based on engraved models from the Recueil d'Architecture by the French architect Jean François de Neufforge The fireplace itself (renewed) is a later addition from the Tuscan period (1806–1814). With the floral bouquets in the ceiling stucco-work, the basket with produce from the sea as a sopraporta relief and the

musical instruments hanging above the door to the adjoining room, the decoration has no uniform theme.

*Painting\*:* Portrait of Prince-Bishop Adam Friedrich v. Seinsheim, Joh. Jos. Scheubel the Younger, 1766.

*Furnishings:* 6 upholstered chairs, Joh. P. Wagner, 1778/1780, painted yellow and silvered to match the room colouring, golden yellow silk damask coverings, renewed, as is the wall covering ■ Commode with three drawers and rounded corners, on six legs, Southern Germany, c. 1785 ■ Dressing table, inlaid with floral marquetry, by Franz Benedikt Schlecht or Johann Georg Fellwöck, Würzburg, c. 1770 ■ Marble group »Pluto abducting Proserpina«, possibly by Joh. W. van der Auvera, Würzburg, c. 1740 ■ Mantelpiece clock shaped like a vase, 18th century, face signed »Johan Michael Henggller« ■ Glass chandelier with crystal pendants.

*Blue Antechamber of the Ingelheim Rooms (Room 35)*

## 35 BLUE ANTECHAMBER OF THE INGELHEIM ROOMS

Apart from the Hall, the Blue Antechamber is the only room in the suite where everything, including the ceiling stucco-work, was redesigned during the redecoration phase of the Seinsheim era in 1776–1778. The stuccoer Materno Bossi based the motifs of the silvered stucco wall decoration on a pale bluish-green background on a design from the Nouvelle Iconologie Historique of Jean Charles Delafosse entitled »Irlande et sa Religion«. The cavettos show martial trophies as do also the decorations in the window jambs, which in addition feature animals from Tiepolo's staircase fresco and thus allude to the four continents. However, the putti in the five reliefs above the three doors, the stove recess and the mirror

\* On loan from the Bavarian State Collection of Paintings, Munich

are by contrast quite unwarlike: they are shown waiting on Diana, goddess of the hunt and thus represent the theme of hunting and fishing. The faience stove from Vienna matches the style of the wall decoration.

*Furnishings:* Seating ensemble, consisting of 8 armchairs and a sofa together with 2 console tables and a table, Joh. P. Wagner, 1776–1778. Painted pale bluish green and silvered, to match the colour scheme of the room; the silk damask coverings of the chairs have been renewed to match the wall covering. The tables were based on a model from the Nouvelle Iconologie Historique of J. Ch. Delafosse entitled »la Perse« ■ Bronze statuette »Jupiter and eagle« from an ancient model, Italy, 17th century ■ 2 sconces, three-armed, cast brass (renovated) ■ Glass chandelier with crystal pendants.

## 36 YELLOW AUDIENCE ROOM OF THE INGELHEIM ROOMS

The stucco decoration of the room again combines the two decoration phases, that of the Regency period under the first patron of the Residence, Prince-Bishop Joh. Philipp Franz v. Schönborn and that of the Zopfstil era under Prince-Bishop Adam Friedrich v. Seinsheim in the 18th century. The stucco-work of the ceiling and the cavetto with the motifs of the sovereignty insignias, fruit and flowers were designed by the stuccoer Joh. P. Castelli to the specifications of the architect Germain Boffrand and produced in 1724/1725. The wall decoration was not added until over 50 years later, by the court stuccoer Materno Bossi, who took up the motifs of the first decoration phase. This is reflected, for example, in the abundant use of floral motifs: the sopraporta reliefs are wreathed with roses, and show putti playing with garlands, above the stove is a flower basket and in the window jambs stuccoed representations of the four seasons.

*Yellow Audience Room of the Ingelheim Rooms (Room 36)*

Here too, Materno Bossi used two models from the *Nouvelle Iconologie Historique* of Jean Charles Delafosse entitled »Moscovie« and »Contrariété«. The faience stove from Vienna matches the style of the wall decoration.

*Tapestries:* 3 tapestries with depictions of country life from motifs by David Teniers. Entrance wall: Peasants at skittles, Brussels, Le Clerc, c. 1710; exit wall: Pastoral scene, Brussels, signed »ACASTRO« (= van der Borght), c. 1710; rear wall: Country fair, Brussels, Le Clerc, c. 1710.

*Furnishings:* 6 armchairs, Joh. P. Wagner, 1776/1780, painted yellow and silvered to match the room, yellow silk damask coverings (renewed) ■ Console table, Joh. P. Wagner, 1772/

1774, painted yellow and silvered ■ 2 commodes, Franconian, c. 1785, veneered in walnut and with various inlays, fittings with porcelain knobs ■ Writing desk with a semicircular closure (bureau à cylindre), Franconian, c. 1780, veneered with walnut, cherrywood and mahogany, inlaid work in a perspective pattern ■ Bust »Truth«, green and white marble with bronze, Pierre François Le Jeune, Stuttgart c. 1776 (signed: »LE JEUNE«) ■ 2 sconces, three-armed, cast brass (renovated) ■ glass chandelier with crystal pendants.

## 37 GREEN CORNER CABINET OF THE INGELHEIM ROOMS

In addition to the stucco-work on the ceiling, for which the stuccoer Joh. P. Castelli was paid in 1725, this room also contains the grey marble fireplace built by the sculptor Peter Heiliger for the First Episcopal Apartment, which is the oldest fireplace in the Residence. It bears the coat of arms of Prince-Bishop Christoph Franz v. Hutten (1725–1729). For the wall decoration of the Seinsheim era, originating in 1776–1778, the stuccoer Materno Bossi used a model from Jean Charles Delafosse's Nouvelle Iconologie Historique entitled »Abissinie ou haute Ethiopie et la Religion«. This is the theme of the decoration around the window opening onto the cour d'honneur in the axis of the suite. Antique bust medallions, fruit baskets and putti playing and making music are the dominant elements of the decoration.

*Furnishings:* 3 armchairs, Joh. P. Wagner, 1776/1780, painted green and silvered to match the room, renewed silk damask coverings ■ Console table, Joh. P. Wagner, 1772/1774, painted green and silvered to match the room ■ Fireplace screen, c. 1780, painted green und silvered, with green silk damask covering ■ Lady's roll-top bureau, Franconian, c. 1770, oak veneered with exotic woods, inlaid in a chequered pattern ■

Wall clock, wood, carved and gilded, probably Franconian c. 1780 ■ Marble group »Nessus and Deianeira«, 18th century ■ 2 sconces, three-armed, cast brass (renewed) ■ Crystal chandelier, Vienna, c. 1750.

## 38 HUTTEN CABINET (NOT ACCESSIBLE)

Ceiling stucco-work by Joh. P. Castelli, 1725, with allegories of the virtues in the corners: Justice, Truth, Temperance and Fortitude, with the coat of arms and the initials of Prince-Bishop Christoph Franz von Hutten (1725–1729) in the lambrequin under the figures. Stucco reliefs above the stove recess and over the door (game birds) by M. Bossi 1776/1778.

## 39 SERVANTS' ROOM
### ADJOINING THE INGELHEIM ROOMS

*Painting:* »Winter landscape« by F.H. Paradyen, c. 1749.

## 40 CHARLOTTE CORRIDOR

The corridor on the northern cour d'honneur side is named after the daughter of King Max I of Bavaria, Princess Charlotte Auguste; she resided in 1815/1816 in the suite then facing the court d'honneur, which had just been furnished by Grand Duke Ferdinand III of Tuscany (1806–1814) for his daughter and which was destroyed in 1945.

# Princes' Hall (Princes' Gallery)

Although situated in the tract constructed from 1726 to 1728 between the two courtyards in the centre of the northern block, the Princes' Hall – originally called the Princes' Gallery – was not completed until 1772. The original plans (1723) for a Court Church here were abandoned. In 1766–1770 the room was provisionally furnished as a music room. – The room decoration was severely damaged in 1945 and completely destroyed above the entablature; restoration was completed in 1978.

*Description of the room:* Oblong room designed as a gallery. Five window axes with windows on both sides. Music balconies at both ends. Walls in white stucco lustro divided by pilasters in the Corinthian style above a wainscot of grey marble. Eight portraits inlaid in the window piers. Elevated entablature area, as a result of converting the round-arched windows (still visible from the outside) into a rectangular form. Continuous cavetto with stucco reliefs by M. Bossi (reproductions), flat ceiling. Fireplace in yellow stucco marble at either end of the room, fireplace mirror, wrought iron rosette grille (atelier of Joh. G. Oegg) on each side of the fireplace, which was opened to let out the warm air from the built-in stoves. Access to the Hall through three of the doors on the narrow sides, the fourth door on the south west leads to the balcony.

As the new representative room of the Seinsheim era, the Princes' Gallery was accordingly much in use: the court used it as a dining room at midday, as a social room for

*State portrait of the last ruler to influence the design of the Residence in the 18th century, Prince-Bishop Adam Friedrich von Seinsheim (1755–1779), by G. Desmarées, 1763/64 (Room 42)*

games and as a concert hall, and gathered here before the opera performances in the adjacent Northern Oval.

The idea for the decoration scheme, which had already been decided on in 1765, originated from Prince-Bishop Adam Friedrich v. Seinsheim himself. The court architects Johann Philipp Geigel and Johann Michael Fischer were responsible for the structural planning, and in 1771/72 the court stuccoer Materno Bossi created the stucco decoration.

Like the staircase, the room is in the goût grec style, a variation of neoclassicism originating from France and popular at the time. The name and significance of the room are derived from the decoration program: eight full-length state portraits of Würzburg prince-bishops – Seinsheim and his seven immediate predecessors – are set in the window piers. These are accompanied in the cavetto by 24 stucco reliefs, in which puttis engaged in various activities symbolize a life free of care under the beneficial rule of these princes.

This was intended to represent the continuous, well-established sovereign tradition and thus also the sovereign claim of the Würzburg prince-bishops at a time when the justification and continuation of the ecclesiastical principalities was being increasingly questioned. The Princes' Gallery is therefore to be interpreted as a memorial to the ecclesiastical principality. It was no coincidence that Adam Friedrich v. Seinsheim had a corresponding room designed for his Bamberg Residence.

Seinsheim's contact with the Munich court played a crucial role in the planning of the Princes' Gallery. In 1764 and 1765, the painter at the Bavarian electoral court, Georg Desmarées, delivered two state portraits to the Würzburg Prince-Bishop. As a result a Princes' Hall was planned, originally in the Northern Oval. François Cuvilliés the Elder delivered a wooden model for this, which is no longer in existence, from Munich in 1766.

When the Opera Theatre was built in the Northern Oval in 1770, this project was abandoned and instead the Princes' Gallery (so named to distinguish it from the hall project) was built in its present location. Cuvilliés' design, which was now invalid because of the change of location and no longer satisfied contemporary tastes, was not used, but the programme concept was retained. One of the portraits of Seinsheim by Georg Desmarées was permanently installed here, while the other was designated for Bamberg.

*Portraits (set in the walls) of the eight prince-bishops:*
Joh. Gottfried v. Guttenberg (reigned 1684–1698)
Joh. Philipp v. Greiffenklau (reigned 1699–1719), painted in 1719
Joh. Philipp Franz von Schönborn (reigned 1719–1724), attributed to J. P Feuerlein
Christoph Franz von Hutten (reigned 1724–1729) by Jo. Ad. Remela (signed)
Friedrich Carl von Schönborn (reigned 1729–1746)
Anselm Franz von Ingelheim (reigned 1746–1749)
Carl Philipp von Greiffenklau (reigned 1749–1754)
Adam Friedrich von Seinsheim (reigned 1755–1779) by Georg Desmarées, 1763/64.

*Furnishings:* 16 armchairs, c. 1780, red silk damask coverings, renewed ■ two chandeliers (new) from models from the Albertina, Vienna.

# Court Chapel (Hofkirche)

## ENTRANCE FROM RESIDENCE SQUARE
## (RESIDENZPLATZ)

### ROOM 43

Although comparatively small, the Hofkirche (Court Chapel) is nevertheless one of the most perfect 18th-century religious buildings in Germany. This high degree of perfection is achieved by both the inspired subtlety of its structure and by the high artistic quality of its decoration. The planning history of this building is long and varied. It was first planned by Balthasar Neumann as a simple rectangular hall in the north-east corner of the Residence, and was then changed by Maximilian von Welsch into an oval central building in the Northern Oval projection; eventually Robert de Cotte moved it to the site of the northern staircase, while Germain Boffrand envisaged it in the transverse wing between the front and back courtyards on the north side.

It was finally located in the south-west corner, in the form designed by Balthasar Neumann in 1730, despite the initial resistance of Prince-Bishop Friedrich Carl von Schönborn, who would have liked to have had it in the south-west pavilion of the cour d'honneur, below his own private apartments. Balthasar Neumann vigorously defended his plans for the Court Church against his rival Lucas von Hildebrandt, who wanted to introduce numerous spatial concepts into the planning – which were however already outmoded. Only the decorations, produced during the years 1735–1743, were designed by Hildebrandt. The architectural concept, above all the highly complex structure of the building, which far exceeds anything Hildebrandt ever created, is exclusively the work of Balthasar Neumann. The pilasters (partial-

*Court Chapel, looking towards the altar*

ly obscured by Hildebrandt's decoration) extend through the entire three storeys of the south-west block, and through eight axes up to the transverse oval.

Aside from the entry portal, the structure of the interior is however in no way reflected by the outer walls. The five oval vaults – a longitudinal oval in the centre, flanked on each side by two transverse ovals – are inserted into the rectangular shape of the interior. The lunettes over the windows and pilasters protrude into the base of the domes, and the domes themselves also intersect to create a rather ambiguous effect. Most important in this is the fact that in spite of the intrusion of the lunettes, the domes still appear as intact ovals in the projection of the ground-plan. It can easily be imagined that the longitudinal oval dome in the centre and the two transverse ovals at the front and back of the church are being broken up by imaginary spatial elements, so that the dome areas only intersect in section, without affecting the completeness of the ovals in the ground plan. As a result, only lunette-like fragments of the two intermediate vaults remain. If instead of starting out from the hollow spaces of the vaults, we concentrate on the structural elements and pillars, what emerge are two broad, ribbon-like bands the thickness of the vault fragments, which converge at their apex; these span the breadth of the church and form, together with the pillars, the supporting structure for the three remaining vaults. The forerunners of this church were not the sacred buildings created by Lucas von Hildebrandt, but rather the work of the brothers Johann and Christoph Dientzenhofer and the younger Kilian Ignaz in Franconia and Bohemia.

Balthasar Neumann's two late masterpieces in Vierzehnheiligen and Neresheim, with which religious architecture culminated in the 18th century, were already anticipated in the design of the Court Church. It is true that the magnificent decoration designed by

»The Assumption of Mary«, altar painting by G. B. Tiepolo, 1752

*Mary Magdalene and two putti at the foot of the cross behind the main altar, stucco sculptures by A. Bossi, 1740/41*

Hildebrandt in many ways spoils the overall structure with the massive but unfortunately horizontal entabla-ture which cuts across the vertical supports of the vault. Here Hildebrandt may, however, have been respecting the wishes of the prince bishop, who wanted an exem-plary court chapel, appropriate for a ruling prince. The inclusion of confessionals was certainly prohibited. Instead oratories were provided and a second altar was installed over the high altar for the daily Mass of Friedrich Carl von Schönborn, whose arms are displayed on the choir loft. Hildebrandt's designs were rendered by Würzburg court artists.

The ceiling frescos, largely reconstructed since the war, were originally painted by Rudolph Byss and his pupils Thalhofer and Högler: over the high altar »The martyrdom of Kilian, apostle of the Franks«, in the centre vault »The Assumption of Mary«, above the choir loft »The fall of the angels«, and on the spandrels the four Evangelists. The stucco decoration and stucco figures, including Christ on the cross with Mary Magdalene in the niche behind the main altar and Mary on the gallery altar, are by Antonio Bossi. The marble sculptures on the high altar (Kilian, apostle of the Franks, on the left and Burkard, the first Bishop of Würzburg, on the right, and those of the side altars (the archangels Raphael and Gabriel with the boy Toby on the left, and the Holy Emperor and Empress Heinrich and Kunigunde) were designed by Johann Wolfgang van der Auvera; some of the preparatory work was probably carried out by Italian sculptors in Carrara. The fine carving is the work of Adam Guthmann (1738), the prie-dieus by Ferdinand Hund (1750). On the side altars are paintings by Giovanni Battista Tiepolo (1752) »The fall of the angels« (left) and »The Assumption« (right). The pulpit in early neoclassical style is by Materno Bossi (1774–1775) and is a later addition. The Court Chapel, especially the frescos in the domes, was severely damaged by fire and water in 1945. The restoration work, which was completed in 1963, is an outstanding achievement.

# Martin von Wagner Museum of the University of Würzburg

OPENING TIMES:

**Gallery**
Tues.–Sat. 9.30 am–12.30 pm

**Antiquities section**
Tues.–Sat. 2 pm–5 pm
Sun. 9.30 am–12.30 pm
Each section open alternate
Sundays

**Graphic Arts Collection**
Tues. and Thurs. 4 pm–6 pm

Entry free of charge.
Tel. (09 31) 31 22 88 or
31 22 83 or 31 28 66
Entrance next to the Court Chapel
in the first southern courtyard

Since 1963 the art gallery of the Martin von Wagner Museum has been housed in the former Episcopal Apartment in the south block. With the antiquities collection on the floor above, it is the largest university museum on the Continent, and was founded in the year 1832 as the university's »aesthetic attribute«. When the son of the court sculptor Joh. P. Wagner, the painter, sculptor, archaeologist and art agent of Ludwig I Martin v. Wagner (1777–1858), donated his important collection of around 10,000 drawings, around 20,000 prints, 36 paintings and around 5,600 ancient works of art to the university in 1857, together with a large sum of money, the study collection of the university, which had been open to the public since 1837, acquired the proportions of a respectable museum and was then named after him. One of the first directors, the music professor Franz Joseph Fröhlich, subsequently donated his own collection of around 300 paintings; today these form the basis of the gallery, which has a total of 580 exhibits. In 1878 the then director Ludwig Urlichs succeeded in acquiring the large and important Feoli collection in Rome, and Würzburg all at once had the third-largest collection of Greek vases in Germany. The museum, which was left with some appreciable gaps after the 2nd World War, continues to benefit from numerous smaller donations. The Graphic

Arts Collection close by with around 25,000 exhibits is in many respects unique. In addition to the approximately 4,000 drawings by Italian artists (including F. Barocci, C. Maratti and C. Marchionni) that he had collected himself during his many years in Rome, M. von Wagner had already inherited a collection from his father. This consists of drawings by important Würzburg court artists, who were engaged here from the 17th to the 19th centuries: Oswald Onghers, Claude Curé, Johann Wolfgang van der Auvera, Clemens Anton Lünenschloß, Georg Anton Urlaub, Joh. P. and Martin Wagner, and finally Giovanni Battista Tiepolo. It also has almost the complete works of Dürer, along with a good cross-section of the most important artists in Europe from the 15th to the 19th century.

## GALLERY
(K-numbers according to the 1986 V. Hoffmann catalogue)

### 1ST CORRIDOR: EARLY ITALIAN PAINTINGS UP TO 1550

The bust of M. Wagner at the entrance is the work of an unknown »Deutschrömer«, one of a particular group of German artists working in Rome, c. 1820. – The large, late Gothic triptych by the Florentine artist »Maestro del Bambino Vispo« (Gherardo Starnina? 1410; K 473) is from Wagner's collection. These excellently preserved panels are a perfect example of the unmixed – and hence intense – colours typical of the Middle Ages. They also show that Wagner was equally interested in all periods of art, not just in classical art.

### ROOM II: LATE GOTHIC FRANCONIAN ART

The finest of the late Gothic works on display here is the early Lamentation relief by Tilman Riemenschneider.

*Central part of
the triptych by
Maestro del
Bambino Vispo,
Florence
c. 1410
(Martin von Wag-
ner Museum,
1st corridor)*

Strong colours and a variety of weaving techniques were used for the large wall tapestry from Nuremberg (K 363). The coats of arms of the Pirckheimer and Watt families and the crucifixion in a style similar to that of the Nuremberg Wolgemut workshop date this work to 1460/65. – A further interesting work is the three-part winged altarpiece opposite, featuring the martyrdom of the Franconian apostles Kilian, Kolonat and Totnan, which was made c. 1490, possibly for the Neumünster church where the tombs of the martyrs are located (K 310). The historically accurate depiction of the Marienberg fortress is unique. – The second Kilian altar, dated 1521, is from the parish church of Mühlhausen near Pommersfelden. It has not been possible to identify the artist responsible for the two wings from a shrine with sculptures which no longer exists (K 185).

## ROOM III: LARGE-SCALE PAINTINGS REPRESENTING ALL SCHOOLS

The right-hand wall shows the development of landscape painting from the dramatic early baroque works of the 17th century to the harmonious compositions of the early 18th century, with works by J.F. Millet (K 320.321), A. Faistenberger (K 148.149), G. Dughet (K 136) and J.F. v. Bloemen (K 30). Three large canvases illustrate the change in Italian historic painting from the splendid calm of Paolo Veronese (K 525) to the almost monochrome, but dramatic compositions of the Neapolitan Luca Giordano (1686; K 204.205). – The unique double portrait (K 380) of an architect with compasses, who appears a second time in the mirror together with the artist, is attributed to, among others, Giov. Battista Paggi from Genoa (1580). It was recently cleaned and preserved in its ruinous condition. Francois Didier Nomé, originally from Metz but working in Naples and

Rome, specialized in imaginary architecture, here with Christ and the woman taken in adultery included in the picture, ca. 1610/20) (K 361).

*»Portrait of Six-
tus Oelhafen«,
painting by Hans
Schäufelein,
c. 1503
(Martin von Wag-
ner Museum,
Room IV)*

The portrait of the imperial official Sixtus Oelhafen (K 437) is attributed to Hans Schäufelein of Nuremberg, and may have been painted in Dürer's workshop, as this work, one of Schäufelein's best, bears traces of Dürer's portrait style. – St Hieronymus by the Nuremberg artist Georg Pencz (1545. K 386), here as a memento mori, is one of the many variations of the Dürer original, painted in Antwerp in 1521 (Lisbon). – The large predella to the left of it, dating from 1627 and depicting the interior of Würzburg cathedral, was produced by the Würzburg court painter Hans Ulrich Bühler for the Bartholomäus altar of the cathedral deacon G. v. Wiesenthau (K 55), shown on the left-hand side of the picture. – The painting of Caritas romana (1546) is by »Meister H.B. mit dem Greifenkopf« (Master H. B. with the griffin head), and is modelled on the self-sacrificing daughter Pero, who suckles her father Cimon, imprisoned and condemned to death by starvation (K 313). – The beech-wood panel, once sawn into pieces, was recently restored and pieced together again. The large panel dated 1514, representing a battle and by an anonymous artist accordingly known as the »Master of the Würzburg Battle« (K 315), is a particularly fine example of German Renaissance art.

The two historical paintings »Mucias Scaevola outside Porsenna« (K 494) and »Coriolanus with the women« (K 495), which Tiepolo must have painted in the winter break 1750/53 (cf. Rinaldo and Armida in the State

Gallery) were probably originally in Balthasar Neumann's collection. The Roman virtues of bravery and generosity (Coriolanus) are here presented in the brilliant colours typical of Tiepolo. – Next to it are two small ruin capricci on goat leather, which were always thought to be by Marco Ricci (1676–1729), the founder of 18th-century Venetian landscape painting. They are now for various reasons ascribed to the younger Francesco Guardi (1712–93; K 404.405). – The magnificent view (1693) of the Quirinal of Rome (K 563) is by Gaspar van Wittel (Vanvitelli), the Roman painter from Amersfoort. – Next to this hangs the veduta signed by Zuccarelli and Visentini in 1746 depicting English palaces in the palladian style, which the English consul Joseph Smith commissioned for his Venetian villa (K 530). – The lifelike portrait of a young nobleman by Sebastian Bombelli of Udine (1635–1719), which shows the influence of Titian and Tintoretto, is from Wagner's collection. – »The Penitent Mary Magdalene« (K 400) by Nicolas Regnier (1590–1667) betrays the Flemish origins of the artist, although he worked mainly in Venice, as well as in Rome.

## ROOM VI: 17TH-CENTURY DUTCH ARTISTS

One of the most striking works in this room is the harmonious, almost monochrome composition »Still Life with Rummers« by Pieter Claesz (1640.K 66). – Contrasting with this puritan severity is the painting by the Flemish artist Franz Wouters (1612–59), which expands on its mythological theme: Zeus in the guise of Diana abducting Diana's companion Callisto, who is later punished for her pregnancy by being turned into a bear (K 564). – The fine portrait of an officer in a leather doublet (K 398) is by Jan Antonisz van Ravesteyn (1570 – 1657) of the Hague. – It is now thought that the large painting showing a canal bank (K 328)and townscape was probably by the younger Frans de Momper (1603–60) rather than by his uncle Joost de Momper. – The Roman landscape with the temple of Minerva Medica dating from 1630 (K 51) is by Bartolomäus Breenbergh (1598–1657), who lived for many years in Rome. – The small, monochrome panel depicting »St Hieronymus in the forest« (K 25), dated 1640, rates as the first signed early work of Nicolaes Berchem of Haarlem (1620–83).

## ROOM VII: 18TH-CENTURY GERMAN PAINTING AND WORKS BY MARTIN VON WAGNER

This room contains works by artists who were active in Franconia, including the Venetian G.A. Pellegrini (1675–1741) who painted the large allegory on the ceiling (from Bensberg Palace; K 385). In addition to paintings by the Franconians G.A. Urlaub (1713–1759) and C. Fesel (1737–1805; portraits of the Treus, an artist couple, K 153.154), the Bavarians Matthäus Günther (1705–88; K 216) and C. Huber (1752–1830) are also represented, the latter with his oil sketch for the ceiling fresco in St Stephan, Würzburg (K 243), which was destroyed in 1945. – In addition to typical landscapes by J.J. v. Cossiau (died c. 1734; K 77), J.F. Beich (1665–1748; K 16) and F. Kobell (1740–99; K 260.261) there are oil sketches by Januarius Zick (1730–97), among them two different drafts for an early work dated 1752: »Saul with the witch of Endor« (K 569), the later version of which has only recently been acquired. The influence of Rembrandt's chiaroscuro, from the same period as Tiepolo's colourful frescoes in Würzburg, is in evidence here. – The remaining walls document Wagner's creativity from 1797–1810 when his huge main work, »The council of the Greeks outside Troy« was completed (1805–08), which was acquired by the young

Bavarian crown prince Ludwig for Munich, marking the start of a life-time friendship between the two men. This giant work (K 556), which has never been sufficiently valued, is Wagner's interpretation of the classicism he encountered with Jacques Louis David in Paris in 1804. Wagner's main piece of sculpture for Ludwig I of Bavaria, the 85-meter marble frieze for the Walhalla (1822–37), is represented with fragments of the plaster models he made for it.

## ROOM VIII: 19TH-CENTURY GERMAN PAINTERS

In the window niche is one of Dannecker's famous clocks decorated with the Three Fates (1794), which was ordered by the Würzburg theologian Franz Oberthür. – Hubert Sattler from Vienna was famous for his »cosmoramas«. In his three pictures the architecture predominates, even if the staffage in front of Westminster Abbey is the coronation procession of Queen Victoria (1838; K 433). – The Ansbach portraitist Johann Friedrich Kreul (1804–67) produced the authentic portrait of the mysterious foundling Caspar Hauser (1830; K 270), who appeared in Nuremberg in 1828 at the age of sixteen and was murdered in 1833. – The sketch of a burial is by the Nazarene Friedrich Overbeck (1789–1869); it was completed in Rome in 1841–45 for St Mary's Church in the artist's home town of Lübeck (K 379). – There is an unusual portrait of Max I Joseph of Bavaria made of feathers, the last example of a »musive painting«, a genre famous at the time which was invented by the Würzburg priest and natural historian Bonavita Blank (1740–1827). This work is by Barbara Thein from Schweinfurt. – Opposite it in a magnificent frame is the recently donated portrait of the Prince Regent Luitpold, who was born in this room in 1821.

## ROOM IX: 19TH-CENTURY GERMAN PAINTERS

The three Italian landscapes by German painters, on whom Italy had a strong influence, are a focal point of this room: Carl Rottmann's wonderful, original Campagna landscape in miniature on a cigar box lid, (1825; K 417), Friedrich Schirmer's large, painstakingly rendered Campagna landscape (1840; K 443) and Oswald Achenbach's later impression of Naples (1890; K 2). – Hans Purrmann's wonderful Florentine landscape was painted in 1935–43 and was bequeathed by Herbert Siebenhüner. – The well-known Munich portraitist Franz von Lenbach painted many portraits of the famous Bavarian theologian Ignaz Döllinger (1799–1890) in Rembrandt's chiaroscuro style (K 286), one of which our museum was able to acquire. – The portrait of Hans Perathoner (1892) by the Würzburg artist Hans Sperlich is a private donation, as are also the two penetrating portraits (1911 and 1923) of the important Würzburg sculptor Fried Heuler (1889–1959).

## ROOM X: 19TH AND 20TH CENTURY GERMAN PAINTERS

Max Liebermann's small, impulsive oil sketch of a seated woman is one of the studies for his Frankfurt work »Free hour in the Amsterdam orphanage« dated 1881 (K 287). – Johann Sperl, a Munich landscape painter, is represented here with his 1892 landscape »Kraiburg am Inn« (K 469). – The room is however dominated by Hans Purrmann's large »Flower piece«, painted by the artist between 1835 and 1843 in Florence for his friend Professor Herbert Siebenhüner, who later worked in this museum and in 1996 left the work to it, together with the fine portrait of the orphan »Guiseppina«. – The bust of Purrmann by the Würzburg sculptress Emy Roeder is the

*Study for »Free hour in the Amsterdam orphanage« by Max Liebermann, 1881*

outcome of a further friendship. Siebenhüner also bequeathed the small bronze figure of a woman with a basket by Emy Roeder. – Loans and donations from the Würzburg artists Josef Scheuplein and Wolfgang Lenz have provided the room with some new features.

## ROOM XI: 20TH-CENTURY ART

The last room focuses on the best of the works that have lately been donated, including many paintings by the Würzburg artists Josef Scheuplein and Curd Lessig. Kurt Michael Voutta's oil painting »I trust to him« (1963) was also a donation, as was the singular, late expressionist painting »In the department store« by Franz

Cestnik (Einbeck 1921, donated c. 1984). The most recent addition, from Paris in 1991, is the oblong abstract painting by Julius Baltazar (Paris 1949). Only Hans Otto Baumann's (1887–1956) large Staffelsee landscape was acquired as long ago as 1933 from the artist, who was living in Würzburg: with its simplification of the subject and its cool colours it is a reflection of the new German realism movement.

## ANTIQUITIES SECTION

### ROOM A: SPECIAL EXHIBITIONS
### ROOM B: EGYPT, EARLY AEGEAN, NEAR EAST

This room contains a small collection of selected ancient Egyptian exhibits, beginning with predynastic times and continuing through to the late period, as well as Cyclades idols, ceramics from Asia Minor and Mycenia, fragments of a tusk helmet, small bronze figures and implements from the Near East (including Luristan), and a glass case with examples of script from Egypt and the Ancient Orient.

### ROOM C: EARLY GREECE

On display are earthenware vessels, terracotta figures and small bronzes from the early history of Greece, beginning with objects from the protogeometric and geometric period (c. 1000–700 BC). Both the shape and decoration of the ceramics of this time are strictly geometric (case C 1 – C 6), with the meander as an important new decorative element. Case C 6 contains geometric objects from a grave, a jug with a lid, various drinking vessels, imitation willow baskets made of earthenware and a pomegranate, symbol of fertility. The two little bronze horses in case C 3, the votive offerings for the gods, and the Boeotian fibula with an engraving of a ship in case C 4 follow the same design pattern as the ceramics.

With the beginning of the Archaic period in around 700 BC, shapes, motifs and modes of representation underwent a change influenced by the Orient. Floral motifs replaced geometric patterns, figures become prominent. There are more regional differences than in the geometric period: Chios made elegant, thin-sided goblets with decoration painted on a white ground (case C 7), Rhodes produced unusual figure vases (case C 9) and the potters' workshops of Corinth created round or pear-shaped ointment bottles decorated with animal friezes in the so-called black-figure style (case C 10). This highly decorative style, an invention of Corinthian vase painters, later spread to the potters' workshops of Laconia (case C 11), Boeotia (case C 13) and Athens (Room D).

*»Satyrs treading grapes« on a Greek wine amphora, c. 540/530 BC (Martin von Wagner Museum, Room D)*

## ROOMS D AND F: BLACK- AND RED-FIGURE CERAMICS OF THE ARCHAIC AND CLASSICAL PERIODS

In the 6th century BC, the potters' workshops of Athens succeeded in perfecting the black-figure style. Their products were exported all over the Mediterranean and were particularly prized by the Etruscans in central Italy, who placed them in graves with their dead. Many of the ceramics in this museum come from these Etruscan graves. They are decorated with a fascinating variety of pictures illustrating the world of the gods and heroes, as well as the everyday life of the Greeks: there are girls fetching water from the well house (case D 17–18) and sportsmen practising under the eye of a trainer (case D 12); Hercules is shown fighting the lion (case D 10) and Aeneas fleeing the burning city of Troy with his father on his back (case D 8), and there are many depictions of the wine god Dionysos with his following of maenads

and satyrs. One of the best black-figure vases in the museum, the amphora (storage jar) by the so-called Amasis painter (case D 9), features plump satyrs plucking and treading grapes (see illustration page 175). Besides the Attic ceramics there is a small but important group of vessels, painted in bright colours and of very high quality, and made, as indicated by the inscriptions in the Chalcidian alphabet, in a Chalcidian workshop. The most beautiful and interesting vessel in this group is probably the large mixing vessel with representations of two couples from the Ilias, Hector and Andromache, Helen and Paris (case D 5).

In around 530 BC a new technique was developed in the potters' workshops of Athens which revolutionised the painting of vases: instead of the figures being painted on, the vases were painted black and the figures pared out of this layer of colour. This red-figure technique, as it is officially called, provided the artists with new ways of representing movement in space. The pictures by the Cleophrades painter in case D 20 (amphora with the departure of a warrior and dancing revellers) and the Berlin painter in case F 4 (amphora with Hercules and Apollo fighting over the Delphic tripod) show how the individual vase painters exploited this new possibility. The preferred drinking vessel at Greek symposia (drinking parties) was the long-stemmed bowl, of which the Brygos bowl (case F 3) is a particularly elegant and artistic example; it is signed by the potter after whom it is named on the inside of a handle. Its humorous, realistic pictures of drinkers enjoying themselves also classify it as one of the masterpieces of Attic ceramics. In the course of the 5th century BC, the style and subject of the pictures changed. While early on there were still dramatic action pictures, such as the unusual depiction of the murder of the Athenean tyrant Hipparch on a wine vessel in case F 6, later in the century these gave way to more peaceful scenes such as that of the ceremonial sacrifice of gods on the amphora in case F 8 or the picture of women making music on a mixing vessel(krater) in case F 10.

## ROOM E: ETRURIA AND CENTRAL ITALY

The room between D and F primarily contains the museum's Etruscan collection. In addition to products of the Protoetruscan Villanova culture (case E 1), it includes the black bucchero vessels typical of Etruria (case E 4) and the imitations of Greek ceramics produced in Etruscan potters' workshops. The so-called Pontic vases from the 2nd half of the 6th century BC, of which the museum has some fine examples, are decorated with particularly original and colourful pictures and indicate an eastern Greek influence (case E 6). There are also Etruscan and Faliscan red-figure painted vessels from the 4th century BC, (cases E 8-9) earthen ash urns, bronze statuettes and implements (case E 10) and two larger than life-sized terracotta deer heads, which were part of the pediment decoration of a temple in Tarquinia.

## ROOM G: SOUTH ITALY. HELLENISM AND
##               ROMAN PERIOD

In the 2nd half of the 5th century BC, Attic potters and vase painters established workshops in the Greek colonies of Southern Italy and Sicily and developed their own style of ceramics with high-quality red-figure painting, which reached its peak in the 4th century BC. Regional styles developed and there are noticeable differences between vases from Apulia (cases G 1-3, G 10, G 13), Campania (cases G 8, G 11–12), Paestum (case G 9) and Sicily (case G 12). The two Apulian vase fragments in case G 17 are unique for what they reveal about ancient theatre and the history of painting, one showing a stage set with accurate perspectives and the other an actor holding a mask (picture on the right), with an expressive contrast between his own appearance and the role he is representing. Vase pictures with representations of phlyakes farce and small earthenware masks and figures of actors (case G 4) round off the picture of the ancient theatre world.

Hellenism, the age between the death of Alexander the Great and the conquering of Egypt by the Romans (323–30 BC) marks the end of the figure-painted ceramics. Characteristic of this period are black-glaze ceramics with stamped patterns or relief decoration, which imitate metal and which could be produced in bulk (case G 6). Room G also has Greek and Roman glasses (case G 16), earthenware figures from Asia Minor (case G 18), findings from graves of the late Egyptian period (case G 19) and Roman ceramic vessels (case G 7).

## ROOM H: GREEK AND ROMAN SCULPTURE

This room, from which there is a fine view of the cathedral, castle and pilgrimage chapel, contains Greek and Roman marble sculpture, including Greek grave reliefs from the classical period and two portraits of Roman emperors (Augustus and Claudius). The oldest and most valuable of the Greek marbles is the head of a centaur from the Parthenon in Athens. In the same case (H 4) is an attractive late classical girl's head from a marble statue that was consecrated in an Attic sanctuary. Dominating the room is a round Roman altar (50 AD), decorated with the reliefs of four winged »putti«, personifying the four seasons (see illustration p.180). The tub-shaped Roman sarcophagus from the middle of the 3rd century, decorated with reliefs which include, on the short sides, the rather unusual motif of elephants, is a

particularly interesting exhibit. Further exhibits include two mummy portraits and, in various wall cases, fragments of Roman decorative reliefs, Greek and Roman bronze statuettes, implements and vessels and Roman glasses.

## ROOM K (RIGHT OF ROOM B): KISELEFF COLLECTION

*Roman »Four seasons altar« made of marble, c. 50 A.D. (Martin von Wagner Museum, Room H)*

This room houses the collection which Dr. h.c. Alexander Kiseleff donated to the University of Würzburg in 1982 and which consists mainly of Egyptian and Greek objects. The comprehensive Egyptian part of the collection contains a good cross-section of almost all types of Egyptian antiquities from the 4th millennium BC to the Christian age: earthenware and stone vessels, sculptures and relief work, fragments of sarcophagi and mummy coverings of cartonage and pearls, Ushabti figures and funerary cones, everyday objects such as toilet articles, tools and games pieces as well as papyrus and small writing tablets. However, the collection's main focus is on jewellery and amulets, with numerous exhibits of excellent quality, primarily made of »Egyptian faience« or glass, but also of gold and decorative stones.

The Greek part of the collection consists primarily of ceramics and terracottas, but also includes objects of glass, bronze and lead, earthenware lamps, two small marble heads and some jewellery. Of particular interest are a colonnette krater painted in black-figure style with Dionysian scenes (case K 28), a Middle Corinthian amphora with an unusual ship painting (case K 36) and a gold diadem from the 4th century BC (case K 31). The collection also includes exhibits from the Minoan civilization, prehistoric objects from Asia Minor and Roman and Etruscan objects.

# Index of Persons

185

# Bibliography

OFFICIAL GUIDE BOOKS

BESCHREIBUNG UND GESCHICHTE DER KÖNIGLICHEN SCHLÖSSER UND LUSTGÄRTEN von Würzburg, Aschaffenburg, Veitshöchheim, Werneck und Bad Brückenau im Unter-Main-Kreise des Königreich's Bayern, von JAKOB MAY, Königl. Bayr. Obersthofmarschall-Stabs-Assessor vorbenannter kgl. Residenzen. Würzburg 1830, pp. 1–49.

OFFIZIELLER FÜHRER durch das Kgl. Schloß Würzburg. Herausgegeben und verlegt vom Kg. Oberstabssekretär G. FRIEDRICH LECHLER, Schloßverwalter in Würzburg. Würzburg 1914 (12. Auflage 1928).

RESIDENZMUSEUM IN WÜRZBURG. Kleiner Führer, herausgegeben von der Direktion der Museen und Kunstsammlungen des ehemaligen Kronguts. (Bearbeiter HEINRICH KREISEL). München 1924.

RESIDENZ WÜRZBURG. Amtlicher Führer. Bearbeitet von HEINRICH KREISEL. Bayerische Verwaltung der staatlichen Schlösser, Gärten und Seen. München 1933 (dritte und letzte Auflage 1939).

RESIDENZ WÜRZBURG UND HOFGARTEN. (Amtlicher Führer). Bearbeitet von ERICH BACHMANN. Erste Nachkriegsauflage München 1970; zweite Nachkriegsauflage 1971; zweite (3.) erweiterte Nachkriegsauflage 1973; zweite (4.) nochmals erweiterte Nachkriegsauflage mit Verzeichnis der Staatsgalerie von ROLF KULTZEN 1975; dritte (5.) Nachkriegsauflage 1976; vierte (6.) Nachkriegsauflage 1978; fünfte (7.) Nachkriegsauflage 1980; sechste (8.) Nachkriegsauflage 1981.

RESIDENZ WÜRZBURG UND HOFGARTEN. (Amtlicher Führer). Bearbeitet von ERICH BACHMANN und BURKARD VON RODA, Verzeichnis der Staatsgalerie von ROLF KULTZEN. Neunte, erweiterte Nachkriegsauflage (revidierte Zählung), München 1982; zehnte, ergänzte Auflage 1988; zwölfte, um das Martin von Wagner Museum erweiterte Auflage 1994; dreizehnte, ergänzte Auflage 2001.

THE WÜRZBURG RESIDENCE AND COURT GARDENS, 11th english edition, München 2003 (entspricht der 13. dt. Nachkriegsauflage 2001).

WÜRZBOURG LE PALAIS DES PRINCES ÉVÊQUES ET LES JARDINS, 6iéme Édition française, München 1999 (entspricht der zwölften deutschen Nachkriegsauflage 1994).

FELIX MADER: Die Kunstdenkmäler des Königreichs Bayern, 3. Band Unterfranken und Aschaffenburg, XII Stadt Würzburg. München 1915, pp. 413–498.

GEORG ECKERT: Balthasar Neumann und die Würzburger Residenzpläne. Ein Beitrag zur Entwicklungsgeschichte des Würzburger Residenzbaues. Straßburg 1917.

HEINRICH GÖBEL: Würzburg und Fulda. Ein Beitrag zur Geschichte der deutschen Wirkteppichmanufakturen im 18. Jahrhundert. Der Cicerone, 12, 1920, pp. 818–823 und 848–856.

KARL LOHMEYER: Die Briefe Balthasar Neumanns an Friedrich Karl von Schönborn, Saarbrücken 1921.

HEINRICH GÖBEL: Das Brüsseler Wirkergeschlecht der van der Hecke. Der Cicerone, 14, 1922, pp. 16–31.

HEINRICH KREISEL: Die künstlerischen Ausstattungen des Hauptstokkes der fürstbischöflichen Residenz zu Würzburg. (Phil. diss. ungedr.), Würzburg 1922.

RICHARD SEDLMAIER und RUDOLF PFISTER: Die fürstbischöfliche Residenz zu Würzburg, München 1923.

HEINRICH KREISEL: Carl Maximilian Mattern, ein Würzburger Kunstschreiner des 18. Jahrhunderts. Der Cicerone 15, 1923, pp. 413–419.
– Die Alexanderwirkteppiche in der Würzburger Residenz, Münchner Jahrbuch der bildenden Kunst, N.F. Band II 1925, pp. 227–249.

FRIEDRICH H. HOFMANN: Das Ehrenhofgitter der Residenz in Würzburg. Zeitschrift für Denkmalpflege, 2, 1927/28, pp. 171–187.

HEINRICH KREISEL: Ein verschollener Hausaltar der Würzburger Residenz. Archiv des Historischen Vereins von Unterfranken und Aschaffenburg, 68, 1929, pp. 520–523.
– Die Kunstschätze der Würzburger Residenz, Würzburg 1930.

ADOLF FEULNER: Die Toskanazimmer der Würzburger Residenz, Zeitschrift für Kunstgeschichte, 3, 1934, pp. 104–108.

THEODOR HETZER: Die Fresken Tiepolos in der Würzburger Residenz. Frankfurt 1943.

HEINRICH KREISEL: Die Würzburger Gobelinmanufaktur und ihre Erzeugnisse. Mainfränkisches Jahrbuch für Geschichte und Kunst, 4, Band 75, 1952, pp. 151–175.

MAX H. VON FREEDEN: Balthasar Neumann, Gedächtnisschau zum 200. Todestage, Ausstellungskatalog Würzburg 1953, Residenz Würzburg.

ERICH BACHMANN: Balthasar Neumann und das Mittelalter, Stifterjahrbuch III, 1953, p. 134.

MAX H. VON FREEDEN und CARL LAMB: Das Meisterwerk des Giovanni Battista Tiepolo (Die Fresken der Würzburger Residenz), München 1956.

LUDWIG DÖRY: Würzburger Wirkereien und ihre Vorbilder, Mainfränkisches Jahrbuch für Geschichte und Kunst, 12, Band 83, 1960, pp. 189–216.

FRITZ ZINCK: Kulturdokumente Frankens aus dem Germanischen Nationalmuseum, Bamberg 1961.

CHRISTIAN BAUER: Der Würzburger Hofgarten, Mainfränkisches Jahrbuch für Geschichte und Kunst, 13, Band 84, 1961, pp. 1–31.

WALTER SCHERZER: Das Staatsarchiv 200 Jahre in der Residenz. Mainfränkisches Jahrbuch für Geschichte und Kunst, 18, Band 89, 1966, pp. 189–198.

CHARLES EDWARD MAYER: The Staircase of the Episcopal Palace at Würzburg. Diss. University of Michigan 1967.

ERICH BACHMANN: Die Würzburger Residenz. Weltkunst, 40, 1970, S. 375 f.

HEINRICH KREISEL: Die Kunst des deutschen Möbels, Bd. II, München 1970.

PETER KOLB: Die Wappen der Würzburger Fürstbischöfe. Würzburg 1974.

GABRIELE DISCHINGER: Die Würzburger Residenz im ausgehenden 18. Jahrhundert. Wiesbaden 1978.
– Der Residenzplatz zu Würzburg – Entwürfe für die Kolonnaden. Mainfränkisches Jahrbuch für Geschichte und Kunst, 30, Band 101, 1978, pp. 93–97.

BURKARD VON RODA: »Laque Martin« in Franken. Jahrbuch der bayerischen Denkmalpflege, 32, 1978, pp. 185–188.

HANS REUTHER: Die Zeichnungen aus dem Nachlaß Balthasar Neumanns. Der Bestand in der Kunstbibliothek Berlin. Veröffentlichung der Kunstbibliothek Berlin, Band 82, Berlin 1979.

FRANK BÜTTNER: Die Sonne Frankens. Ikonographie des Freskos der Würzburger Residenz. Münchner Jahrbuch der bildenden Kunst, 3. Folge, Band 30, 1979, pp. 159–186.
– Giovanni Battista Tiepolo. Die Fresken in der Residenz zu Würzburg. Würzburg 1980.

KARL SCHÄFER: Johann Prokop Mayer 1735–1804. Ein Würzburger Hofgärtner. Mainfränkisches Jahrbuch für Geschichte und Kunst, 32, Band 103, 1980, pp. 165–176.

BURKARD VON RODA: Adam Friedrich von Seinsheim, Auftraggeber zwischen Rokoko und Klassizismus. Zur Würzburger und Bamberger Hofkunst anhand der Privatkorrespondenz des Fürstbischofs (1755–1779). Quellen und Darstellungen zur fränkischen Kunstgeschichte, Band 6, Neustadt/Aisch 1980.

MAX H. VON FREEDEN: Balthasar Neumann, Leben und Werk, 3. Auflage, München 1981.

JOACHIM HOTZ: Das »Skizzenbuch Balthasar Neumanns«. Studien zur Arbeitsweise des Würzburger Meisters und zur Dekorationskunst im 18. Jahrhundert. 2 Bände. Wiesbaden 1981.

HANS-PETER TRENSCHEL: Meisterwerke fränkischer Möbelkunst. Carl Maximilian Mattern. Würzburg 1982.

HANS REUTHER: Balthasar Neumann. Der mainfränkische Barockbaumeister. München 1983.

ROBERT MÜNSTER: Die Melodien einer Bamberger Pendule aus dem Jahre 1750. Musik in Bayern, Heft 26, 1983, pp. 29–34.

BURKARD VON RODA: Der Frankoniabrunnen auf dem Würzburger Residenzplatz. Jahrbuch für fränkische Landesforschung, 43, 1983, pp. 195–214.
– Höfische Interieurs. Innenräume des Rokoko und Empire aus der Residenz Würzburg, Kunst und Antiquitäten, 1984, Heft 6, pp. 44–51.

ERICH HUBALA und OTTO MAYER: Die Residenz zu Würzburg. Würzburg 1984.

ERICH HUBALA: Genie, Kollektiv und Meisterschaft – zur Autorenfrage der Würzburger Residenzarchitektur. In: Martin Gosebruch zu Ehren. Hrsg.: Frank Neidhart Steigerwald, München 1984, pp. 157–170.

IRENE HELMREICH-SCHOELLER: Empiremöbel in Würzburg. Sitzgarnituren aus den ehemaligen Toskanazimmern der Residenz. Kunst und Antiquitäten, 1985, Heft 3, pp. 60–66.

HANS REUTHER: Die Konstruktion der Treppenarme im Stiegenhaus der Würzburger Residenz. In: Intuition und Darstellung. Erich Hubala zum 24. März 1985. Hrsg. von Frank Büttner und Christian Lenz, München 1985. pp. 241–250.

BURKARD VON RODA: Aus Würzburger Hofbesitz, Säkularisationsgut in Münchner Sammlungen, Kunst u. Antiquitäten,1985, Heft 3, S. 52–59.
– »Das Spiegelzimmer im königlichen Schloß zu Würzburg.« An interior painted by Georg Dehn and a report by Georg Dollmann commissioned by Ludwig II of Bavaria. In: Furniture History, 21, 1985, pp. 107–120.

WILFRIED HANSMANN: Balthasar Neumann – Leben und Werk. Köln 1986.

BERNHARD SCHÜTZ: Balthasar Neumann, Freiburg 1986.

IRENE HELMREICH-SCHOELLER: Die Toskanazimmer der Würzburger Residenz. München 1987.

HANS-PETER TRENSCHEL: Das Spiegelkabinett der Würzburger Residenz. In: Altfränkische Bilder und Wappenkalender 86, Würzburg 1987, pp. 15–19.

AUS BALTHASAR NEUMANNS BAUBÜRO: Pläne der Sammlung Eckert zu Bauten des großen Barockarchitekten. Sonderausstellung aus Anlaß der 300. Wiederkehr des Geburtstages Balthasar Neumanns. Mainfränkisches Museum Würzburg. Ausstellungskatalog Würzburg 1987.

SAMMLUNG ECKERT. Plansammlung aus dem Nachlaß Balthasar Neumanns im Mainfränkischen Museum Würzburg. Unter Mitverwendung der Vorarbeiten von Joachim Hotz bearbeitet von Hanswernfried Muth, Elisabeth Sperzel und Hans-Peter Trenschel. Mainfränkisches Museum Würzburg (Hg.) Würzburg 1987.

STEFAN KUMMER: Balthasar Neumann und die frühe Planungsphase der Würzburger Residenz. In: Thomas Korth und Joachim Poeschke (Hg.), Balthasar Neumann, Beiträge zum Jubiläumsjahr 1987, München 1987, pp. 79–91.

BERNHARD SCHÜTZ: Fassaden als Weltarchitektur. Die Würzburger Residenz. In: Thomas Korth und Joachim Poeschke (Hg.), Balthasar Neumann, Beiträge zum Jubiläumsjahr 1987. München 1987, pp. 92–112.

ANNEGRET VON LÜDE: Studien zum Bauwesen in Würzburg 1720 bis 1750. Würzburg 1987.

ALBRECHT MILLER: Die Residenz in Würzburg. Königstein im Taunus, 3. Aufl. 1990.

BARBARA STRIEDER: Johann Zick (1702–1762) – Die Fresken und Deckengemälde. Worms 1990.

KATHARINA FEGG: Die fürstbischöfliche Wandteppichmanufaktur zu Würzburg 1721–1779. In: Mainfränkisches Jahrbuch für Geschichte und Kunst 43, 1991, pp. 8–79.

VERENA FRIEDRICH: Johann Georg Oegg: Die schmiedeeisernen Gitter der Fürstbischöflichen Residenz zu Würzburg. Würzburg 1993.

BERND M. MAYER: Johann Rudolf Bys (1662–1738) – Studien zu Leben und Werk. München 1994.

SVETLANA ALPERS UND MICHAEL BAXANDALL: Tiepolo and the Pictorial Intelligence. New Haven/London 1994 (deutsch 1996).

PETER O. KRÜCKMANN (Hg.): Der Himmel auf Erden – Tiepolo in Würzburg. 2 Bde., München/New York 1996.

BETTINA SCHWABE und SONJA SEIDEL: Drei Supraporten von Domenico Tiepolo. In: Restauro 102, 1996, pp. 320–327.

THORSTEN MARR: Restaurierung und Wertschätzung – Giovanni Battista Tiepolo und die Fresken der Würzburger Residenz. In: Mainfränkisches Jahrbuch für Geschichte und Kunst 49, 1997, pp. 157–166.

MATTHIAS STASCHULL: Das Deckenfresko im Treppenhaus der Würzburger Residenz von Giambattista Tiepolo – Ein Beitrag zur Restaurierungsgeschichte. In: Bayerische Schlösser - Bewahren und Erforschen (= Bayerische Verwaltung der staatlichen Schlösser, Gärten und Seen, Forschungen zur Kunst- und Kulturgeschichte, hrsg. von Gerhard Hojer, Bd. V), München 1996, pp. 289–298.

ARNO STÖRKEL: Der Mann mit dem Pferd und Neumann auf dem Kanonenrohr. Eine Studie zur Identifikation zweier Personen in Tiepolos Würzburger Treppenhaus. In: Mainfränkisches Jahrbuch für Geschichte und Kunst 49, 1997, pp. 141–156.

JARL KREMEIER: Die Hofkirche der Würzburger Residenz. Worms 1999.

IRIS VISOSKY-ANTRACK: Materno und Augustin Bossi. München/Berlin 2000.

## PRESERVATION AND RECONSTRUCTION

RUDOLF ESTERER und HEINRICH KREISEL: Instandsetzung und Ausgestaltung der staatlichen bayerischen Schlösser in Franken. Deutsche Kunst und Denkmalpflege, 1934, pp. 2–20 (hier S. 2–7).

OTTO HERTWIG: Die Wiederherstellung der Tiepolo-Fresken in der Residenz Würzburg. Österreichische Zeitschrift für Kunst und Denkmalpflege, 6, 1952, pp. 57–63.

JOHN D. SKILTON jr: Würzburg 1945, Erinnerungen eines amerikanischen Kunstschutz-Offiziers. Würzburg 1954.

KARL KÖRNER: Zur Instandsetzung der Würzburger Hofkirche. Deutsche Kunst und Denkmalpflege, 1962, pp. 47–52.

LARS LANDSCHREIBER: Sicherung des Vestibüls, des Treppenhauses und des Weißen Saales in der Residenz Würzburg. Deutsche Kunst und Denkmalpflege, 1968, S. 87–91.
– die neue Farbgebung im Treppenhaus der Würzburger Residenz. Ebenda, p. 92 f.

OTTO MEYER: Kritik und Rechtfertigung nach 25 Jahren Wiederaufbau. Würzburg heute, Zeitschrift für Kultur und Wirtschaft, 1970, pp. 122–126

HEINRICH KREISEL: Die Wiederherstellung und Einrichtung der südlichen Paradezimmer in der Würzburger Residenz. Kunstchronik, 23, 1970, pp. 173–176.
– Wiedereröffnung der »Weißen Zimmer« in der Würzburger Residenz. Kunstchronik, 25, 1972, pp. 353–357.

HEINZ LÜTZELBERGER: Der Wiederaufbau der Würzburger Residenz am Beispiel der Ingelheimer Zimmer und des Fürstensaals. Schönere Heimat, 68, München 1979, Heft 1, pp. 15–21

ERICH HUBALA und OTTO MEYER: Die Residenz zu Würzburg. Würzburg 1984.

# SEHENSWÜRDIGKEITEN DER
# BAYERISCHEN SCHLÖSSERVERWALTUNG

INFORMATIONEN

| Ansbach | **Residenz der Markgrafen von Ansbach** Prunkappartements des frühen Rokoko, Sammlung Ansbacher Fayencen und Porzellan, Hofgarten mit Orangerie | ☎ (09 81) 95 38 39-0 FAX (09 81) 95 38 39-40 |

Aschaffenburg

**Schloss Johannisburg**
Gemäldegalerie und Kurfürstliche Wohn-
räume, Sammlung von Korkmodellen,
Schlossgarten;
Städtisches Schlossmuseum

☎ (0 60 21) 3 86 57-0
FAX (0 60 21) 3 86 57-16

**Pompejanum**
Nachbildung eines römischen Hauses und
Antikenmuseum

**Schloss und Park Schönbusch**
Klassizistisches Schlösschen in
englischem Landschaftsgarten

Bamberg

**Neue Residenz Bamberg**
Kaisersaal und barocke Prunkräume,
Gemäldegalerie, Rosengarten

☎ (09 51) 5 19 39-0
und (09 51) 5 19 39-1 13
FAX (09 51) 5 19 39-1 29

**Schloss Seehof**
Stilräume, Rokokogarten, Kaskade mit
Wasserspielen

Bayreuth

**Neues Schloss**
Markgrafenresidenz aus der Zeit des
»Bayreuther Rokoko« mit Museum
Bayreuther Fayencen,
Hofgarten mit Orangerie

☎ (09 21) 7 59 69-0
FAX (09 21) 7 59 69-15

**Markgräfliches Opernhaus**

Burg
Lauenstein
Ludwigsstadt

Schloss
Rosenau
Coburg
Veste Coburg
Schloss Ehrenburg
Kulmbach

85
Plassenburg
Burg Zwernitz Felsengarten
Sanspareil
Neue Residenz
Bamberg
Bamberg
Bayreuth
Schloss Eremitage
Markgräfliches Opernhaus
Neues Schloss Bayreuth
Schloss Fantaisie

mpejanum
Schloss Johannisburg
Aschaffenburg
Schloss
chönbusch
Würzburg
Schloss Veitshöchheim
Residenz Würzburg
Alte
Hof-
haltung
Schloss
Seehof

Festung
Marienberg

Main

7

3

73

Schnaittach
9
Festung
Rothenberg

Nürnberg
Tucherschlösschen
Kaiserburg
Nürnberg

93

Residenz
Ansbach
Ansbach
7
6

3

Residenz
Ellingen
Weissenburg
13
Regensburg

Riedenburg
Rosenburg
Befreiungshalle Kelheim
Willibalds-
burg
Burg
Prunn
Kelheim
3

Eichstätt
Donau
93
Schloss Neuburg
Neuburg

92
Isar

Dillingen
Schloss
Höchstädt
Landshut
Stadtresidenz
Landshut
Burg Trausnitz

Neu-Ulm
Augsburg
8
Schloss Lustheim
Schloss Dachau
Schloss Schleißheim
Englischer Garten
Burg
Burghausen
9
12
Schloss
Nymphenburg
Residenz München
München
Ruhmeshalle und Bavaria
Künstlerhaus Gasteiger
Ammersee
Lech
Starnberger
See
Schloss
Herrenchiemsee
Chiem-
see
Künstlerhaus
Exter
8
Residenz
Kempten
Kempten
Staffel-
see
Tegern-
see
Forggen-
see
Schloss Linderhof
Füssen
Ettal
Garmisch-Partenkirchen
St. Bartholomä
Königs-
see
Bodensee
Lindau
Schloss
Neuschwanstein
Königshaus
am Schachen

| | | |
|---|---|---|
| Bayreuth/<br>Donndorf | **Gartenkunst-Museum Schloss und**<br>**Park Fantaisie** | ☎ (09 21) 73 14 00-11<br>FAX (09 21) 73 14 00-15 |
| Bayreuth/<br>Eremitage | **Altes Schloss Eremitage**<br>Wohnräume der Markgräfin Wilhelmine,<br>Grotte, historische Gartenanlage mit<br>Wasserspielen | ☎ (09 21) 7 59 69-37<br>FAX (09 21) 7 59 69-41 |
| Bayreuth/Wonsees<br>Sanspareil | **Felsengarten u. Morgenländischer Bau**<br>Stilräume, Gartenparterre und Felsengarten | ☎ (0 92 74) 33-0<br>oder 12 21 |
| | **Burg Zwernitz**<br>Burganlage | |
| Burghausen | **Burg zu Burghausen**<br>Burganlage, Stilräume, Gemäldegalerie | ☎ (0 86 77) 46 59<br>FAX (0 86 77) 6 56 74 |
| Coburg | **Schloss Ehrenburg**<br>Historische Wohn- und Prunkräume des<br>Barock und 19. Jahrhunderts | ☎ (0 95 61) 80 88-0<br>FAX (0 95 61) 80 88-40 |
| Coburg/<br>Rödental | **Schloss Rosenau**<br>in englischem Landschaftsgarten,<br>Wohnräume der Biedermeierzeit und<br>neugotischer Marmorsaal | ☎ (0 95 63) 30 84-0<br>FAX (0 95 61) 30 84-29 |
| Dachau | **Schloss Dachau**<br>Festsaal, Hofgarten | ☎ (0 81 31) 8 79 23<br>FAX (0 81 31) 7 85 73 |
| Eichstätt | **Willibaldsburg**<br>Festungsanlage, Juramuseum,<br>Ur- und Frühgeschichtsmuseum,<br>Bastionsgarten | ☎ (0 84 21) 47 30<br>FAX (0 84 21) 81 94 |

| Ellingen | **Residenz Ellingen** | ☎ (0 91 41) 9 74 79-0 |
| | Prunkappartements des Fürsten Wrede, | FAX (0 91 41) 9 74 79-7 |
| | Deutschordensräume, Schlosskirche, | |
| | historischer Park | |
| | | |
| Herrenchiemsee | **Neues Schloss Herrenchiemsee** | ☎ (0 80 51) 68 87-0 |
| | Wohn- und Repräsentationsräume, histori- | FAX (0 80 51) 68 87-99 |
| | sche Gartenanlage mit Wasserspielen und | |
| | **König Ludwig II.-Museum** | |
| | | |
| | **Museum im Augustiner-** | |
| | **Chorherrenstift Herrenchiemsee** | |
| | **(Altes Schloss)** | |
| | Dauerausstellung zur ehemaligen Klosteran- | |
| | lage u. zum Verfassungskonvent; Stilräume | |
| | König Ludwigs II; Gemäldegalerie J. Exter | |
| | | |
| Höchstädt | **Schloss Höchstädt** | ☎ (0 84 31) 88 97 |
| | Kapelle mit Sammlung | FAX (0 84 31) 4 26 89 |
| | südwestdeutscher Fayencen | |
| | | |
| Holzhausen | **Künstlerhaus Gasteiger** | ☎ (0 88 06) 26 82 |
| | Sommervilla mit Wohnräumen und | |
| | Werken von Anna und Mathias Gasteiger, | |
| | Landschaftsgarten | |
| | | |
| Kelheim | **Befreiungshalle** | ☎ (0 94 41) 6 82 07-0 |
| | | FAX (0 94 41) 6 82 07-7 |
| Kempten | **Residenz Kempten** | ☎ (08 31) 2 56-2 51 |
| | Prunkräume und Thronsaal der Fürstäbte | FAX (08 31) 2 56-2 60 |
| | | |
| Königssee | **St. Bartholomä** | ☎ (0 80 51) 9 66 58-0 |
| | Jagdschloss, Kapelle St. Johann und Paul, | FAX (0 80 51) 9 66 58-38 |
| | Naturpark Berchtesgaden | |

| Kulmbach | **Plassenburg**<br>Schöner Hof, historische Markgrafenzimmer, Gemäldegalerie, Jagdwaffensammlung | ☎ (0 92 21) 82 20-0<br>FAX (0 92 21) 82 20-26 |
| Landshut | **Stadtresidenz**<br>Stilräume und Gemäldegalerie | ☎ (08 71) 9 24 11-0/-44<br>FAX (08 71) 9 24 11-40 |
| | **Burg Trausnitz**<br>Burganlage mit Burgkapelle St. Georg, Stilräume | |
| Lauenstein bei<br>Ludwigsstadt | **Burg Lauenstein**<br>Burganlage, Wohnräume,<br>volkskundliche Sammlungen | ☎ (0 92 63) 4 00<br>FAX (0 92 63) 97 44 22 |
| Linderhof | **Schloss Linderhof**<br>Wohn- und Repräsentationsräume,<br>Venusgrotte, Marokkanisches Haus,<br>Maurischer Kiosk, Hundinghütte und<br>Einsiedelei des Gurnemanz,<br>historische Gartenanlage mit<br>Wasserspielen | ☎ (0 88 22) 92 03-0<br>FAX (0 88 22) 92 03-11 |
| München | **Residenz München und Hofgarten**<br>Historische Wohn- und Prunkräume aus<br>der Zeit der Renaissance bis zum 19.<br>Jahrhundert, Hofkirchen und -kapellen,<br>Spezialsammlungen (Silber, Porzellan,<br>Paramente, Reliquien) | ☎ (0 89) 2 90 67-1<br>FAX (0 89) 2 90 67-2 25 |
| | **Schatzkammer der Residenz** | |
| | **Cuvilliés-Theater** | |
| | **Feldherrnhalle** | |

**Ruhmeshalle und Bavaria**
auf der Theresienhöhe

**Schloss Nymphenburg**      ☎ (0 89) 1 79 08-0
Prunk- und Stilräume, Festsaal,      FAX (0 89) 1 79 08-6 27
Schönheitengalerie, Schlosskapelle

**Amalienburg, Badenburg,**
**Pagodenburg, Magdalenenklause**
im historischen Schlosspark

**Marstallmuseum**
Höfische Kutschen und Schlitten,
Reit- und Sattelzeug

**Museum Nymphenburger Porzellan**
Sammlung Bäuml

**Englischer Garten**      ☎ (0 89) 3 86 66 39-0
Landschaftsgarten im englischen Stil      FAX (0 89) 3 86 66 39-23

München/      **Neues Schloss Schleißheim**      ☎ (0 89) 31 58 72-0
Oberschleißheim      Festsäle, Staatsappartements,      FAX (0 89) 31 58 72-50
Gemäldegalerie, barocker Hofgarten

**Schloss Lustheim**
Museum Meißener Porzellan

Neuburg a.d.      **Schloss Neuburg a.d. Donau**      ☎ (0 84 31) 88 97
Donau      Sgraffitofassade, Kapelle, Grotten; Vorge-      FAX (0 84 31) 4 26 89
schichte Pfalz-Neuburg, Kirchlicher Barock

Neuschwanstein/      **Schloss Neuschwanstein**      ☎ (0 83 62) 8 10 35
Schwangau      Wohn- und Repräsentationsräume      und (0 83 62) 8 18 01
      FAX (0 83 62) 89 90

| | | |
|---|---|---|
| Nürnberg | **Kaiserburg Nürnberg**<br>Palas, Stilräume, Doppelkapelle, Tiefer<br>Brunnen und Sinwellturm, Burggarten | ☎ (09 11) 22 57 26<br>FAX (09 11) 2 05 91 17 |
| Prunn im<br>Altmühltal | **Burg Prunn**<br>Stilräume | ☎ (0 94 42) 33 23<br>FAX (0 94 42) 33 35 |
| Riedenburg | **Burg Rosenburg**<br>Burganlage mit Kapelle;<br>privat betriebener Falkenhof | ☎ (0 94 42) 27 52<br>FAX (0 94 42) 32 87 |
| Schachen | **Königshaus am Schachen**<br>Wohnräume und Türkischer Saal,<br>Alpengarten | ☎ (01 72) 8 76 88 68<br>und (0 88 22) 92 03-0<br>FAX (0 88 22) 92 03-11 |
| Schnaittach | **Festung Rothenberg**<br>Ruine einer Festungsanlage aus dem<br>18. Jahrhundert | ☎ (0 91 53) 77 93 |
| Übersee/Feldwies | **Künstlerhaus Exter**<br>mit Atelier des Malers Julius Exter | ☎ (0 86 42) 89 50-83<br>FAX (0 86 42) 89 50-85 |
| Veitshöchheim | **Schloss und Park Veitshöchheim**<br>Historische Wohnräume,<br>Rokokogarten mit Wasserspielen | ☎ (09 31) 9 15 82 |
| Würzburg | **Residenz Würzburg**<br>Barocke Prunkräume, Fresken von<br>G. B. Tiepolo, Gemäldegalerie, Hofgarten | ☎ (09 31) 3 55 17-0<br>FAX (09 31) 5 19 25 |
| | **Festung Marienberg**<br>Festungsanlage, Fürstenbaumuseum mit<br>Schatzkammer, Paramentensaal und<br>stadtgeschichtliche Sammlungen,<br>Maschikuliturm, Fürstengarten;<br>Mainfränkisches Museum | |

# VERÖFFENTLICHUNGEN DER BAYERISCHEN SCHLÖSSERVERWALTUNG

Deutsch, teilweise auch in englisch, französisch, italienisch und japanisch erhältlich

## Amtliche Führer

| | |
|---|---|
| Ansbach | Residenz Ansbach |
| Aschaffenburg | Schloss Aschaffenburg; Pompejanum in Aschaffenburg |
| | Schloss und Park Schönbusch |
| Bamberg | Neue Residenz Bamberg |
| Bayreuth | Eremitage zu Bayreuth |
| | Markgräfliches Opernhaus Bayreuth |
| | Neues Schloss Bayreuth |
| Bayreuth/Wonsees | Felsengarten Sanspareil – Burg Zwernitz |
| Burghausen | Burg zu Burghausen |
| Coburg | Coburg – Schloss Ehrenburg |
| Coburg/Rödental | Schloss Rosenau |
| Dachau | Schloss Dachau |
| Eichstätt | Willibaldsburg Eichstätt |
| Ellingen | Residenz Ellingen |
| Herrenchiemsee | Neues Schloss Herrenchiemsee |
| Kelheim | Befreiungshalle Kelheim |
| Königssee | St. Bartholomä am Königssee |
| Kulmbach | Plassenburg ob Kulmbach |
| Landshut | Landshut Burg Trausnitz; Stadtresidenz Landshut |
| Lauenstein bei Ludwigsstadt | Burg Lauenstein |
| Linderhof | Schloss Linderhof |
| München | Residenz München; Schatzkammer der Residenz München |
| | Altes Residenztheater in München (Cuvilliés-Theater) |
| | Englischer Garten München; Ruhmeshalle und Bavaria |
| | Nymphenburg, Schloss, Park und Burgen |
| | Marstallmuseum in Schloss Nymphenburg |
| Neuburg a. d. Donau | Schlossmuseum Neuburg an der Donau |
| Neuschwanstein/Schwangau | Schloss Neuschwanstein |
| Nürnberg | Kaiserburg Nürnberg |
| Oberschleißheim | Schloss Schleißheim, Neues Schloss und Garten |
| Prunn | Burg Prunn |
| Riedenburg | Burg Rosenburg in Riedenburg an der Altmühl |
| Schachen | Königshaus am Schachen |
| Veitshöchheim | Schloss Veitshöchheim und Hofgarten |
| Würzburg | Festung Marienberg zu Würzburg |
| | Residenz Würzburg und Hofgarten |

A free list of all the Bavarian Palace Department's publications and the publications themselves (for which there is a charge) can be ordered from

Bayerische Schlösserverwaltung
Postfach 380120 • 80614 München
Tel. (089) 17908-165 • Fax (089) 17908-190
Info@bsv.bayern.de • www.schloesser.bayern.de

The present eleventh English edition corresponds to the thirteenth German postwar edition of 2001. It takes over from the previous editions the main part of the text by *Erich Bachmann*, the sections on the Northern Oval Gallery Hall and the Ingelheim Rooms by *Burkard von Roda*, the description of the Mirror Cabinet, which was reopened in 1987, and rooms 11–13a by *Werner Helmberger*, the section on the State Gallery by *Annette Kranz* and the brief description of the Martin von Wagner Museum of the University of Würzburg with texts by *Tilman Kossatz*, *Theodor Zauzich* and *Irma Wehgartner*.

Picture credits:
Artothek/Jochen Remmer (Bayerische Staatsgemäldesammlungen): S. 124 – Brandl, Anton J.: U1, S. 2, 4, 7, 8, 18, 35, 40, 42, 44–45, 65, U4 (Putto) – Martin von Wagner Museum: S. 164, 167, 172, 175, 179, 180 – Mülbe, Wolf-Christian von der: 12, 13, 25, 56–57, 60–61, 63, 68, 70–71, 73, 74 – All others: Bayerische Schlösserverwaltung/Mayr, Herrmann, Scherf u. a. – Gartenplan: Norbert Nordmann

Translation revised by Sue Bollans

11th edition
© Bayerische Verwaltung der staatlichen Schlösser, Gärten und Seen, Munich 2003
Graphic design: Verena Fleischmann, Munich
Design and setting of the service section: Frese, Munich
Lithography: Reproline, Munich
Printed by Passavia, Passau
ISBN 3-932982-47-9
Printed in Germany

# Numbered Garden Plan

1 Residence
2 Cour d'honneur
3 Franconia Fountain
4 Court Chapel
5 Court Garden gate next to the
   Ambassadorial Building
   (Georg and Anton Oegg)
6 Ambassadorial Building (restaurant)
7 Residence Square (Residenzplatz)
8 Rosenbachhof (state wine cellar)
9 Rosenbach Park
10 Greiffenklau gate by the
   Rennweg (Georg Oegg)
11 Northern Court Gar-
   den gate (Georg
   Oegg)
12 East Garden, laid
   out within and on
   top of a bastion
   of the Baroque
   town wall
13 Parterre with
   lawn, pool,
   flowerbeds
   and rose
   gardens,
   surrounded by
   pergolas made of cornelian
   cherry and larch trees with groups of
   cast putto figures by Peter Wagner
14 Terrace on the tip of the bastion,
   balustrade with cast sculptures by
   Peter Wagner
15 South Garden: Parterre with lawn,
   flowerbeds, fountain and cone-shaped
   yew trees, with sculptures under them
   by Peter Wagner (copies). The monumental sculptures »Abduction of Europe«
   and »Abduction of Proserpina« on the
   sides were also originally by Peter Wagner (now replaced by sandstone copies)

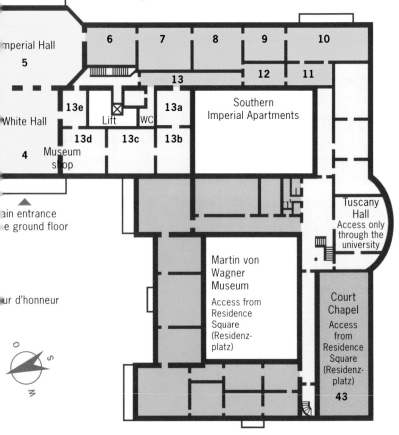

# Würzburg Residence main floor

1 Vestibule (ground floor below 4)
2 Garden Hall (ground floor below 5)
3 Staircase
4 White Hall
5 Imperial Hall

6–10 Southern Imperial Apartments
6 Antechamber
7 Audience Room
8 Bedroom/Venetian Room
9 Mirror Cabinet
10 Gallery

11 Servants' Room
12 Servants' Room
13 Corridor
13a–e Connecting rooms (Shop, Cafeteria

14–21 Northern Imperial Apartments
14 Antechamber
15 Audience Room
16 Red Cabinet
17 Green Room
18 Bedroom
19 First Guest Room
20 Second Guest Room

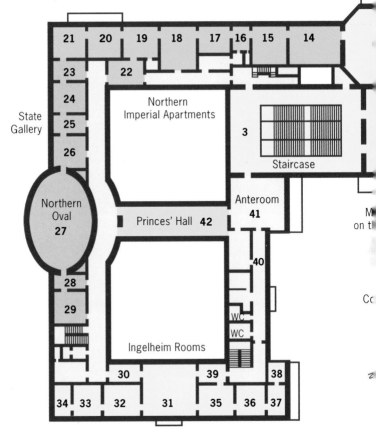

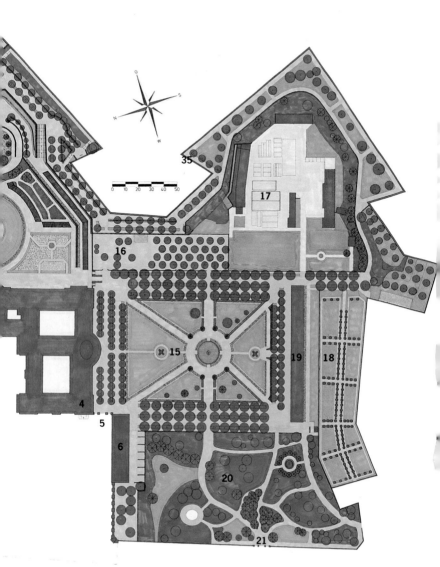

16 Lime tree gallery with an open area
    for musical performances
17 Nursery (not accessible)
18 Kitchen garden
19 Orangery

20 Landscape Garden
21 Court Garden gate on the Promenade
    (G. Oegg)
22 Access to the gardens from Otto-
    straße